FAN TALES

A CHRONICLE OF
WILD TURKEY HUNTING STORIES

BERDETTE ELAINE ZASTROW

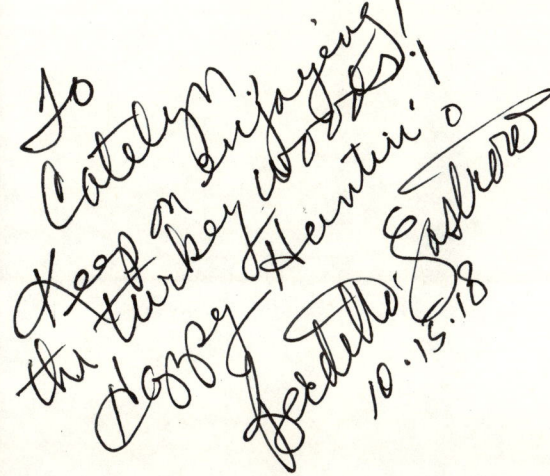

To Catelyn,
Keep on enjoying
the turkey woods!
Happy Huntin'
Berdette Zastrow
10-15-18

Print ISBN: 978-1-54394-015-2

eBook ISBN: 978-1-54394-016-9

Wild Outdoors Publications
bzastrow@venturecomm.net
Grenville, South Dakota 57239
Printed in the United State of America

DEDICATION

This book is dedicated to new spring wild turkey hunters, whether they are 10 or 80. May you enjoy the most awesome of hunts which will reward you with satisfaction, wonder, thankfulness, frustration, good grub and lots of fun.

Thanks to God for the wonderful creation He has given us, the knowledge and ability to recognize how special nature is and especially for granting us the wonder and passion of wild turkeys.

I've always said, "Wild turkey hunting should come with a warning label: Danger! May turn participant into a fanatic!"

Berdette Elaine Zastrow

TABLE OF CONTENTS

FOREWARD

There are few things that stir the hunter's soul
like the gobble of a wild turkey during the spring.
Especially when that gobble is heard in the pine for-
ests of the Black Hills of South Dakota. For several
years I had the privilege of accompanying Berdette
on spring turkey hunts in those very Black Hills for-
ests. I witnessed a true conservation dedication from
the joy of taking her first turkey to resource management for all wildlife species in South Dakota.

I met Berdette while she served on the South
Dakota Game, Fish and Parks Commission. As a
big game biologist that often testified to the commission, I was impressed with her knowledge and
willingness to listen to all sides in management of
natural resources in South Dakota. She worked dil-
igently with national conservation organizations
such as the Rocky Mountain Elk Foundation and the
National Wild Turkey Foundation. For example, she
was instrumental in introducing the Eastern subspecies of the wild turkey into available habitats in
South Dakota.

One of Berdette's major accomplishments was helping start the Women in the Outdoors program in South Dakota. Berdette recognized the largely untouched potential of female hunters and their ability to affect natural resource management.

Most of all, I have valued the friendship that developed with Berdette. It has been a privilege to listen to that turkey gobble at first light with a true sportswoman.

Les Rice
Former SD Game, Fish and Parks Big Game
Biologist, Turkey Hunting Guide

SPECIAL TRIBUTES

Thank you:

to all who suggested these tales be published and for the encouragement and support to accomplish it,

to all categories of wild turkey hunters who taught me, accompanied me and appreciated fun and excitement in the turkey woods and enhanced my hunts,

to all who consented to be a part of this publication and

special thanks to Robin Matushin, my cheerleader and proofreader.

INTRODUCTION

One of the most interesting and fulfilling experi-ences in my life was serving on the South Dakota Game, Fish and Parks Commission for eight years. Loving the outdoors was extremely enhanced through my friends and contacts while serving. "Falling into the turkey hunting world" was coincidental and is precious to me. It started on a plane ride to a commission meeting.

Art Talsma, wildlife biologist, started a discussion about turkey hunting. He suggested I attend a National Wild Turkey Federation convention to learn what turkey hunting was all about. Les Rice was the Big Game Biologist in charge of turkey management in South Dakota and was a huge fan of turkey hunting and its promotion. His addiction to the big birds was contagious. Having waterfowl and pheasant hunting under my belt, and discovering how much fun hunting in general was, I desired to learn more about this crazy turkey hunting.

Attending the convention lighted a fire which has not diminished in over twenty-eight years. After talking turkey with many people, hearing calls and seeing enthusiasm I'd never seen before or after for ANYTHING, I couldn't wait to hunt the elusive wild turkey. Needing to be outfitted properly, friends at the convention helped me purchase camouflage clothing, calls and more which I needed for my new foray into the woods. I was intrigued at every turn. Turkey calls, especially, grabbed my attention at the convention.

While standing in the middle of an aisle I heard funny noises but couldn't discern where they were originating. Deciding a gal in a nearby display booth was making the noise, I stared at her. She never moved a muscle, not hands, head or mouth. I was stunned. Where was the noise coming from? It finally dawned on me. Now I knew what diaphragm mouth calls were. Attending the convention certainly did its job. I was hooked and had to get into the turkey woods.

FAN TALES chronicles my exciting journey through first learning how to turkey hunt, learning to call and hunt by myself and receiving the most meaningful enjoyment teaching and guiding others into the world of wild experiences and fun of spring and fall wild turkey hunting.

Curl up by the fire, lay lazily in a boat or hammock, or as you are waiting for the big boy to come in to your decoys, travel along with me in the turkey woods and share laughs and experiences with me as I relive my special turkey tales with some of my turkey-lovin' buddies.

CHAPTER ONE

THE LADY GETS HER BIRD

Spring of 1990 I was faced with skepticism rang-ing from my family asking "You are going where to do what?" to my walking into turkey hunt headquarters in the Black Hills of South Dakota hearing conversations stop and seeing disbelieving faces. I had to persuade everyone I was serious. I was going to hunt wild turkeys in the beautiful Hills and planned to get a bird, my first ever, if luck was with me. At the time, there were few female turkey hunters.

I was no stranger to hunting. I hunted pheasants as a teenager and still enjoy the fall outings. Waterfowl season caught my fancy in the fall of 1989, and no one was more proud than me to have my own geese on the table. Now, it was time for the big game bird—wild turkey.

As a South Dakota Game, Fish and Parks commissioner, I was involved in many wildlife activities and eager to learn more about our great South Dakota resources. Attending the NWTF (National Wild Turkey Federation) convention in Nashville in 1988 was informative, fun and inspiring. I knew I would someday be a wild turkey hunter.

The day I received an invitation to the 5th Annual Governor's Invitational Black Hills Wild Turkey Hunt I let out a yelp that would've startled a turkey five miles away. The hunt was to take place in early May following a commission meeting in Rapid City. Sitting still through the meeting was tough, but as I found out, good training for the sitting and patience needed for the hunt. Finally, it was time to leave for turkey camp, the Covered Wagon at Piedmont, on the eastern edge of the Hills.

After introductions at camp, checking into my room and changing into complete dressed-to-kill camouflage, I was ready, or so I thought. But it wasn't until after camo taping my shotgun, shell dispersion, being outfitted with a vest, a seat cushion and proper face mask and much advice I was ready. My mentors didn't care for my red-framed glasses, but they were all I had.

With adrenaline pumping and spirits soaring, I was on my way to bag my bird. As one of the only, if any, females ever to be at this turkey camp at the time, I felt the pressure. I had something to prove to myself and I also knew I was being watched. When Bo Hauer, my guide, told me his success rate was 100 percent, my stomach did a flip. Would I be accepted? Would I be taken seriously? Could I really do this?

While sitting on a ridge during the afternoon hunt and waiting out a rainstorm, Bo answered many questions I had. When the rain stopped, we climbed and walked and Bo called and we sat. At least these activities were good for stress and they calmed me down. No turkeys gobbled so we headed back to camp.

After a fine meal, it was show-and-tell hunting story time. All the guys who had bagged birds that day had the supreme pleasure of repeating the hunt to a very attentive audience. Successful hunters had a trophy feather tucked in a NWTF cap. Talk about envy! The pressure was on. I *had* to get a bird the next morning as I planned to leave for home in the afternoon.

When the alarm rang at 3:00 a.m. the next morning, I was thinking positive: *Watch out gobblers, here I come!* We climbed, we sat, Bo called, we listened, we walked and walked and repeated all this for hours. Nothing responded.

On the way back to camp, we saw some toms strutting for a few hens down by a corral when we drove over a ridge. Bo tried to call them in, but they liked what they had better than what they heard. I'm sure it had nothing to do with the fact I adjusted my face mask at a most inopportune time. It was a silent trip back to camp.

Ten minutes back in camp dispelled my worry about being accepted and taken seriously. Everyone's interest in my hunt surprised me. They asked all kinds of questions and I saw these guys genuinely cared about me getting my first bird.

They helped me pattern my shotgun after lunch and those experts said, "it would have been a dead bird" and "shooting turkeys is easier than shooting geese." Becoming more excited, I decided to stay another day.

We crawled into Bo's Jeep at four o'clock in the afternoon. The hills weren't strangers to me any longer, but by then, they looked like 18,000-foot peaks. Since it's completely flat where we farm in northeastern South Dakota, the mountain climbing was testing. Eventually, following Bo through the brush, woods and up the mountains, listening to his various calls finally became routine and my back-rest trees were almost comfortable. I dozed several times, lulled by sounds of nature, dreaming of shooting a big bird.

Suddenly, "howl, screech!" Bo's predator call woke up everything in the forest, but still no turkey talk. We heard a few gobbles across a far ravine, but that was it.

The evening in camp was a rerun of the evening before with turkey stories. Although I was disappointed myself, I was happy for the other hunters.

Rob Keck, executive vice president of the NWTF at the time, presented special turkey hunt certificates and other awards. Harvey Rattey, sculptor and turkey hunter from Bozeman, Montana, graciously donated a beautiful bronze turkey sculpture, "Lil' Gobbler," which was generously presented to me. I was thrilled, but by that time thought it would be the only bird I'd take home. I'll never forget the camaraderie of that evening. Turkey hunters have some inner chemistry forging them together.

After the story telling, there was some type of small conference in the kitchen with Bo and Bill Hearne, turkey hunter from Black Hawk, South Dakota, as the center of attention. Then, the announcement was made. A turkey was put to bed in a canyon, and I was going to get to work that bird in the morning. The pressure was really on now. It was my last hunt of the last day. With all the hunters rooting for me, I had to get the bird.

Sleep did not come easy for the few hours allowed me and upon rising, I psyched myself up for this last, most desperate hunt for the elusive wild turkey. Applying camo makeup at 2:30 a.m. is not my favorite thing to do, but I wanted everything perfect. Shells were double-checked and my gun was re-taped. I walked out the door whistling the tune from "Bridge on the River Kwai." I was ready.

We spoke in hushed tones as we drove toward the canyon. I now had two guides and they were determined to make sure I had a chance to bag that tom. Bill stayed close to the vehicle, while Bo and I walked 400 yards up a road, then up a steep ridge. Bo pointed at "my" tree and I sat down.

The gobbler was still snoozing in a ponderosa pine close by. Both Bo and Bill repeatedly told me it was extremely important to be absolutely still because of a lack of cover in front of me. It took a few minutes to get settled as tree roots were poking up at the base of the tree and the steep slope made it difficult to become comfortable.

I remembered how, during previous hunts, the excitement drifted away, and then I was occupied only with survival—to blot out the stiffness and numbness of quietly sitting. Bo's father had told me how to exercise muscles without moving, which helped dispel the numbness. I tried it but my foot slipped down the ridge some. I feared if I saw a turkey and moved my leg I'd roll down the slope and shoot myself. My confidence in seeing a turkey, or even hearing one, waned as negative thinking tried to bubble to the surface.

I daydreamed, thinking about all the other creatures I saw who didn't see me. I thought about catching myself nodding off against a large tree trunk at 4:30 a.m., never having done that before. What a good feeling it was to really get down, dirty, sweaty and one-on-one with an earthy nature. I thought of my father who took me fishing but assumed a girl would never be a hunter. I thanked God for letting me live in such a beautiful state, and I ….*gobble, gobble, gobble.* The hairs stood up on the back of my neck! Adrenaline surged inside me. *That was a turkey—two of them.*

Being alert took on new meaning and the numbness disappeared. For the very first time ever, I was listening to a wild turkey gobble. Soon I heard a quiet, calm, but very insistent hen call behind me as Bo was talking to the tom. I was fascinated listening to the conversation while watching dawn break over the Black Hills. Ponderosa pines holding turkeys were silhouetted against a dark blue sky accented with oranges and pinks and the distant hills were kissed in purple.

As I listened I wondered how long they gobble before they fly down. A few minutes more, and I heard the unmistakable wing beats of a turkey flying to the ground. This was getting serious and I was ready to panic. I wondered how long after they hit the ground can you see them? I thought I had asked all the important questions. Thirty seconds later, I spied movement. Both gobblers were running along the road. One peeled off and ran up the ridge—my side of the ridge.

Sweat ran down the middle of my back as I watched him run up, wondering how and when I would get a good shot. When the bird stepped out from behind a tree only 15 yards in front of me in full strut it was one of the most beautiful sights I'd ever seen. But was I supposed to shoot? He was so beautiful he caught me off guard. I was told he would simply move his head out from behind a tree and then it would be over. This was something else. I watched and waited, trying to anticipate his next move. He looked at me, his feathers went down and he charged. *Now what do I do?*

I sat still, frozen. *He's going to jump in my lap!* When he got within six yards of me, he stopped. He stared. What a shock to him to find this funny-looking animal with red glasses instead of a new girl friend. *Do I shoot now? He's too close. He's looking at me! I can't shoot him in the face!*

After he figured he'd see no action here, he turned slowly and started up the ridge. Bo whispered "shoot" and the turkey caught on. His legs started moving and that's when my gun did, too. As he came out from behind a tree stump, one shot made him history. Bo let out a whoop and ran up the ridge to get him. Me? I was in a state of shock and couldn't move.

Finally, on shaky legs, I managed to stand up and take a look at my wild turkey. He was the most spectacular thing I'd ever seen and he was mine.

Hearing rustling in the brush, I spied Bill on the way up the ridge giving hearty congratulations. "Here's your shell," he excitedly said as he handed over a spent 12-gauge shell. He continued, "It's the same shell. I know because I marked it." Not comprehending what he was saying, I asked him what he meant. It turned out to be quite a story.

The first day at camp the guys didn't like the shells I brought so they gave me some of theirs. Bill, whom I had never met until then, set one shell on the table saying it would be the shell to kill my bird. I thought, *sure,* but it was a nice gesture and I threw it in my ammo bag with the rest of the shells.

The next morning while loading my gun in the dark, I just happened to grab Bill's marked shell and insert it in the gun first. Amazingly, that was the shell that downed my first tom. Bill also kept stats. The first gobble was at 4:50 a.m., he flew down at 5:15 and the shot was fired at 5:17. He gobbled 101 times, weighed 16 pounds and nine ounces, had 5/8-inch spurs and an 8½-inch beard.

Walking in the door back at camp, my legs hurt, my bottom was stiff and I was still shaking, but when I walked out of the woods with that beautiful Merriam's slung over my shoulder, I felt nine feet tall. My heart was bursting with pride. As I was told later, yes indeed, this was a classic hunt. And, yes indeed, I did fall in love with the magnificent wild turkey and turkey hunting in the wonderful Black Hills of my South Dakota.

So began my love and passion for wild turkey hunting.

Guide Bo Hauer and author's first wild turkey.

CHAPTER TWO

THE CROWN ROYAL BIRD

I felt proud as a peacock as I sauntered into the same turkey camp in the Black Hills a year later. Greetings were profuse at Turkey Tracks Ranch, run by John and Bo Hauer. I was thrilled Les Rice, Game, Fish and Parks big game biologist at the time, would be my guide.

"We're gonna get you a Crown Royal bird, girl," Les sleepily announced as we pulled out of the camp. "I put a nice guy to bed in my favorite hunting spot last night so I know exactly where he is."

I tried to keep up with Les as we shuffled along in the dark, walking uphill for only part of the way. After quietly swishing through tall grass, Les stopped and indicated my hunting spot beside a Ponderosa pine. Les sat immediately behind me. Then, it was the big wait.

The lightest of pink seeped into the eastern sky and we heard gobbles echoing through the hills. Suddenly, a piercing gobble cut the air directly over our heads. I jumped. As I slowly turned my head to grab a look at Les behind me, his eyes seemed to be frozen wide open. He quietly whispered, "Dammit, we are right under the roost tree! You really have to sit still."

He was mad because he had miscalculated and gotten too close. If the gobbler had even an inkling we were right underneath him, he would fly down on the opposite side of the tree and run away. Of course, I was still learning and had all the confidence in the world in Les and his calling.

He made the softest, sweetest hen yelps only a few times, just to let the bird know a "hen" was down there. Gobbles rocked us again. I was sitting as still as I possibly could. I was scared to breathe. Then, they appeared—mosquitoes—buzzing and zipping around my head. My hunting mask better be adjusted correctly or the little devils would find their way inside the mask and I didn't dare move to slap them. Although surprisingly quiet, I soon heard "slap" behind me. Three more slaps and I was getting mad at Les.

At the same time, a couple mosquitoes found their way inside my mask. I was horrified. What could I do? I didn't dare move. I forced myself to settle down and started thinking about exactly how painful, really, was a biting mosquito? After all, if I made it through the pains of childbirth twice, I ought to be able to stand a couple bugs biting me. So, I sat it out, gritting my teeth as they bit and giggling inside about my guide slapping his face. Who's the macho one here?

Totally engrossed with the mosquitoes, I failed to hear the gobbler fly down. Les nudged my arm and said to look to my right. There was the tom, twenty yards away, parading through the tall grass looking for his "hen." His mistake was stretching his neck and showing off that brilliant red head. It was quickly all over for him.

Les's rule is "the guide carries out the game." We laughed so hard we had to stop various times on the way to the vehicle as we relived the hunt, complete with mosquito slaps.

"I told you this was gonna be a Crown Royal bird, so let's do it," Les cheered as we drove back into camp. I still had no idea what he was talking about. "Wait here, I'll be right back," he said as he told me to wait on the porch.

Finally, here he comes, bringing two mugs of coffee. "Here is your Crown Royal coffee for your Crown Royal bird," he toasted. What an introduction to Crown Royal whiskey!

*Les Rice, guide,
and author with the Crown Royal bird.*

CHAPTER THREE

MORE LES
RICE ADVENTURES
A LESSON
FOR THE FUTURE

The first time I shot my gobbler while with Les, he jumped up and down, yelled and really celebrated the shot. He did the same thing on the second hunt, creating a loud disturbance in the woods when my bird hit the ground. I finally asked him about it.

"Why are you so excited when I shoot a bird?" I asked. "After all, I was the one who shot him. So why are you so hyper?"

With a serious look, directly in the eye, he answered. "Believe me, after you have shot enough birds yourself, it is much more exciting to take someone else out hunting, especially a first-time hunter or a young hunter. You just wait. This will happen to you. You will jump and scream just like me. You will find it's a bigger thrill to guide someone else than to get your own bird."

"Aw, shucks, that will never happen to me," I told him.

Wrong. He was correct. I have more fun taking others than shooting a bird myself these days. I have to stop and think at application time—do I even want a tag for myself?

A BAD CALLER

It was mid-afternoon and we were trekking through the Black Hills. Stopping and intermittently throwing out a call or two, we worked our way through the forest, hearing nothing. Deciding on taking a little rest, we settled in under a Ponderosa pine tree and listened to the quiet, grateful for the wonderful opportunity to be there.

Les yelped a couple times. Nothing. Suddenly, a raspy, goofy-sounding noise came from behind us. "Another hunter," Les whispered. The calls persisted, the last progressively worse than the first. And the sound became louder. We wondered why the other hunter was walking and calling, or rather, squawking. He'd never get a bird in that way.

A few minutes more of the racket echoed through the trees. The caustic noise was coming up on our left and we were just about to start talking loudly so the hunter would know we were there.

Suddenly, a big Merriam's hen strutted by. We were shocked into silence, and then started laughing. She was the caller, the most terrible caller we had ever heard. No more worrying about perfectionism while giving hen yelps. We still laugh about the "croaking hen."

THE PRONE BODY

We were perched on a rocky ridge with a huge meadow below us. We decided to watch for birds picking their way through the grass. Les gave up a few hen yelps, and then we'd sit and wait and listen. Nothing was cooperating and the meadow remained empty, but then, a poke in my ribs. Les nodded his head forward. Expecting a flash of black and white feathers and seeing none, I couldn't see what he was stirred up about.

Finally, I saw it—what looked like a prone human body, with a shotgun on his lap, laying beside rocks below us. We sat and watched what seemed like forever and the guy didn't move. Oh geez. Was he alive? Do we scare him by hollering at him? Would we wake him up? (Taking a nap while in turkey woods is quite a common thing.) We simply waited. No movement. Les got up, walked down to the man and started talking to him.

The guy didn't turn his head right away, in fact, he did nothing but a nod to acknowledge Les's presence. After a few words, Les came back with a peculiar look on his face.

"The guy is a deaf hunter," he calmly said. We sat and thought about the implications for a bit, deciding it was a very dangerous situation. Silently, we quickly left the spot. I don't know why we were so quiet—the guy couldn't hear us anyway.

UNCLE DON'S HUNT

Now, I should probably introduce you to my Ol' Uncle Don, as he is known in our hunting circles. He is my mother's little brother, who is more like a big brother to me than an uncle. When my father was in the Army in World War II, my mother and I lived with her parents. Uncle Donnie babysat me, read me stories and was my hero. He taught me how to shoot a BB gun on my grandparent's farm when I was six years old and we have been close all my life. He is humorous, always joking, pulling pranks and we have always had a lot of fun together. He retired from DuPont about the same time I learned how to hunt and we have been hunting together ever since. He also supplies much fodder for my writings.

Well, Ol' Uncle Don wanted to learn how to turkey hunt. At the time, the Black Hills was our only turkey hunting arena. I called Les and we were on our way out west.

Les was to pick us up at our hotel in Rapid City at 2:30 a.m. our first day. It was pouring rain and

Les had a long face when he arrived. "The birds will hold tight, they won't talk, it will be miserable, so we should stay put for today," he told us.

I hadn't driven over 300 miles to be told to stay in because of a little rain. I insisted we go and we went, loaded down with rain gear. Les grumbled but we trudged through the mud because "we came to hunt."

Our first set-up was under a birch tree. True to his prediction, no turkeys answered Les's yelps. However, there was a pair of magpies in the tree above us. The rain certainly didn't bother them. They made a lot of noise and crashed through the tree back and forth. I disgustedly asked Uncle Don what they were doing. Wrong thing to ask. I still remember his answer, but it won't be printed here.

Les led us up a steep ridge when the rain slowed down. As we peeked over the top, we saw two gobblers with nine hens below us, doing their thing. Turkeys are like us. They don't like to walk uphill, and with the light rain, Les whispered to us. "They will never come up here. This is impossible. There are NINE hens down there with them."

After declaring our confidence in Les and his calling, he grudgingly agreed to try to talk to the birds, muttering "this won't work." We hunkered down and waited.

Les is a fantastic turkey caller. He sounds like he IS a bird. He started yelping, explicitly giving them putts, clucks and more. He got their attention—hens' and the gobblers'. A few more soft yelps and lo and behold, the two gobblers were on their way up the ridge in the rain. They conveniently walked in front of Uncle Don's and my shotguns and they were history.

This hunt and calling feat proved to us Les Rice was and still is, one of the best darn turkey callers on this earth.

Les Rice insisted
"the guide always carries the bird out."

CHAPTER FOUR

WEST RIVER BIRDS

West River landowner-hunter relationships in South Dakota could be volatile at times. Harding County, in extreme northwest South Dakota, had the reputation of being a "boiling pot of emotions." However, the conservation officer there, Brian Meiers, readily contained minor explosions and prevented situations from getting worse. He was also a good friend, hunter and turkey caller. At Brian's invitation, Ol' Uncle Don and I had a fun turkey hunt, although it was quite different.

After scouting for a few hours the first afternoon and "paying our dues," Brian suggested we head to a particular farm where the big birds hung out. Being on a short time-table, we accepted the offer. While we were loading shotguns, adorning ourselves with vests and masks, Brian took a peek in the small feedlot behind a barn. He stealthily came back, saying there were two big gobblers standing by the fence, only 30 yards from the corner of the barn. We planned our strategy.

My uncle would take the one on the right and I'd take the one on the left.

Well, "the best laid plans…." We silently crept to the barn corner. Instead of waiting for the "1,2,3 shoot" as we usually do, over-excited Ol' Uncle Don blasted away before I got to the corner. "Boom!" Both turkeys hit the ground and I never made a shot. Being a little miffed is putting it mildly. To be legal, I had to use my tag for the second bird. I was not happy and my Ol' uncle received a very stern sermon.

I couldn't remain mad at him as we had another hunt planned in the southern Black Hills and I would have to ride 300 miles home with him. He is also of the demeanor which makes it hard to stay mad at as he's always joking.

That was the only time I turkey hunted with Brian, but he and Mike Smeltzer, another West River conservation officer, guided me to my cow elk in Custer State Park a few years later for an awesome hunt.

CHAPTER FIVE

CUSTER STATE PARK TURKEYS

I've always loved South Dakota's jewel, Custer State Park. Long-legged John Wrede, conservation officer at the time in Rapid City, offered to help me hunt gobblers in the park. He is also a great caller, but trying to keep up with his long legs covering lots of ground, mostly uphill, was difficult. I was delighted for any rest I got.

Layering clothing is the norm for turkey hunting and working up a good sweat dictated I remove one layer as we reached a tall ridge overlooking a previous forest burn. I'll never forget the look on John's face when I announced "I'm taking my sweater off."

His eyes widened, he looked embarrassed and quickly turned his back to me. I couldn't help but giggle to myself. What in the heck did he think I was going to do? Strip in the woods?

When I told him I was ready to move on again, he slowly turned around, peeking to see if I still had a top on. He gave me a sheepish grin and said "ok" as he started out again.

Part way up another ridge, a gobble reverberated through the forest. We hit the ground and I settled in beside a big Ponderosa pine. John's expert hen yelps and clucks brought the hormone-ridden guy in to me and the shot connected. The hunt was fun, of course, and in a beautiful setting, but one of the most memorable hunts of all occurred on a later hunt in the park.

A LESSON LEARNED

The most memorable hunts can be the hunts when you harvest nothing but the experience. It's the "being out there" in nature and having funny things happen, learning wildlife lessons firsthand and conquering challenges you have assigned to yourself. The following hunt will remain the funniest of my life and is completely unforgettable.

At 0-dark-thirty we climbed a trail which started in Custer State Park's Coolidge Inn parking lot and then angled up a hill behind the complex. We crossed a small stream while listening to some jakes as we trudged up the incline. They were in a tree about 60 yards from us and we heard them fly down. Suddenly, we heard a gobble behind us, back down the hill. We quickly and quietly chose our set-up spot. Two trees growing as one with the crotch as a backdrop behind my shoulders was the perfect spot to view a small area about 60 yards below me.

John sat 50 yards up the hill behind me to call and encourage the bird to look past me for the "hen." The tom was strutting, drumming and spitting and provided a nice Black Hills show. All was going well. The tom was answering John's hen calls and the jakes were providing background turkey music behind us. However, there was one problem.

A fallen log lay about 20 yards downhill from me. It was there I learned the hard way how turkeys walk around an obstruction, like the log, instead of jumping over it. He pranced around down beyond the log, stubbornly refusing to come up the hill to me. In a few minutes, he was out of sight. After being so seriously instructed in making no movement, I did not turn my head to see where he was. I thought he would suddenly appear right in front of me. He still answered hen yelps but I couldn't see him.

John continued calling and the gobbler carried on the conversation, but I was extremely frustrated because I couldn't see the bird. I didn't know what to do. Finally, not spying a hen, the tom shut up and disappeared. John had worked so hard to bring him to me, and somehow I must have botched the hunt. I felt bad and figured John would be angry.

All of a sudden, I heard the jakes and their raspy gobbles again. I guessed they were answering John all the time we worked the big tom, but I was so engrossed with the tom I didn't pay attention to them. John continued calling and they answered, becoming closer with every hoarse gobble. I did not want to shoot a jake, but at this point, I thought, why not?

Sitting and listening to the jakes come closer and closer, my adrenalin clicked in again. They sounded close behind me, still trying to gobble like the big boys. I waited for what seemed like forever and I couldn't take it anymore. They did not walk out in front of me, so I knew I had to turn around. On the count of three, I turned and had the surprise of my life.

Three jakes were immediately behind my tree, standing and all looking at me through the crotch of the tree, almost sitting on my shoulders and burst forth with resounding loud gobbles right in my face! I jumped two feet, dropped the gun and tried to regain my breath. As they quickly ran away, I looked up at John. He was holding his sides, almost rolling down the hill with laughter.

OK, so I was outwitted not once, but two times by these dang Black Hills Merriam's. Following our recovery, John then told me my big tom had walked up the hill way to my left, walked around the log, had been within gun range, saw no hen and vamoosed in the woods.

"Why didn't you turn your head?" John asked. "You could've shot him!" Then, feeling terrible, I answered I was told not to move. "Well, you can slowly turn your head to see where he is!" OK. Since then, I very slowly turn my head and haven't been caught yet. What a lesson to learn the hard way. But, those jakes have provided years of laughter and I relive it every turkey season.

CHAPTER SIX

A CHANGING
POPULATION

Historically, Merriam's turkeys populated the Black Hills and some were transplanted in northeast South Dakota in the 1960s. Rio Grande birds, originally stocked in the 1960s, also populated the same northeast South Dakota area for decades. Due to increasing populations resulting in depredation complaints from landowners in the northeast, Game, Fish and Parks biologists decided to import Eastern turkeys into the area.

Eastern birds are extremely wary and less inclined to inhabit farmyards and make nuisances of themselves. It sounded like a win/win proposition. In the fall of 1996, twenty-six Eastern sub-species hens were brought into the area from Missouri and released near Veblen and Sica Hollow in Marshall and Roberts Counties. Biologists studied population numbers for five years before the first hunting season opened.

Chad Lehman, then an SDSU graduate student, was the "attending physician." He literally lived with the birds year round, researching everything there was to know about the resident population.

I became acquainted with Lehman and was interested in all aspects of the population. It was especially fun to "hunt for poults" in early summers, finding radio-collared hens and then seeking their nests and counting young. By participating in these activities, an appreciation of turkeys' lives grows. Nesting can be difficult, depending on spring weather in northeast South Dakota. Predation on nests by coyotes, raccoons and skunks commonly took place. Thinking of all the negatives, it's a wonder any poults survive. However, turkey hens are great mothers and poults are survivors.

It was on one of these poult-finding excursions Lehman invited me to hunt with him, whenever the season opened. The idea of hunting in an area where Eastern birds would be hunted for the first time was extremely exciting. Along with a professional who literally lived with the birds and could make every possible sound a turkey can make, the season promised to be an exhilarating experience.

On one of the first days of the open spring season, we planned a hunt. "I know where they will roost, so we'll set up in a spot along their way," Lehman announced as we drove to the hunting area for an evening hunt.

Another new aspect of turkey hunting at this time was added during this first foray into Roberts County—use of a gobbler decoy. No one used turkey decoys when I first started hunting the birds, but after the first one was successfully deployed in the woods, decoy sales and use skyrocketed.

The decoy idea is based on turkeys' fantastic eyesight. I was told a turkey "can see a tick on a log 300 yards away," which means they can certainly see exactly where a call is coming from, hence the "sitting still" part. Decoys raise the hunters' chances of harvesting a bird, but the hunter still has to remain motionless, quiet, aware and ready.

Now, back to the hunt. Lehman was excited this was his first hunt in the new season with the "new" turkeys and brought a video recorder (VHS tape at that time) to capture the experience. He was very excited to have a documented hunt of "his" birds. Lehman placed his gobbler decoy about 25 yards in front of me in a dry shallow stream bed as I nestled in front of a large tree. I thought the video recorder may interfere with the hunt, such as a gobbler hearing it, seeing a red light, etc. There was nothing to fear as Lehman began calling--not simply a yelp or cluck, but all kinds of turkey sounds, many of which I had never heard at the time, and still have never heard. His repertoire was unbelievable and I admired his talent and knowledge.

Soon, a resounding gobble hit our ears. The bird was out about 100 yards and gobbles echoed through the trees as he ran in to us along the stream bed, never stopping until he saw the decoy. He was a beautiful Merriam's, not an Eastern, but I didn't care. He pranced, he danced, he strutted and put on quite a performance for us and the decoy. Never having seen this action before, I'm sure my eyes were huge and I could hardly breathe.

I waited and watched, drinking in this wonderful show. I'm sure Chad was ready for a heart attack because I didn't shoot right away. It was simple: I wanted to watch the show. And, to know this was being recorded on video added to the fun. I'd have this show forever and could watch it the rest of my life.

Finally, I pulled the trigger and the show was over. Chad and I both let out a yell to shouts of "What a show!" I was thrilled and so was he. At photo time, we posed the bird just right for a few shots. Then Chad said he wanted to interview me and obtain my thoughts and excitement on video to provide a great ending to the hunt.

I was ready and Chad paused. His face fell. He folded and sunk to the ground. "I pushed the wrong button," he sorrowfully drawled. "I have nothing of the hunt recorded."

Oh no! The "show" was completely gone, only to be replayed in our heads. No video, no audio, nothing. We sat in silence. Well, at least, it wasn't my fault. Trying to console Chad, I maintained a positive attitude and we continued on with an "after the hunt" interview. Honestly, I didn't need it on tape. The hunt is indelibly engraved in my mind.

As of this writing, Dr. Chad Lehman is now Wildlife Biologist stationed at Custer State Park. Asked if he remembers our hunt, I always receive a "yes, of course." And then he reminds me my bird was the first one harvested in that particular unit when it was opened. What fun we've all had since that inaugural hunt.

Thanks to Chad and his talented work with wild turkeys, we have great populations of birds in northeast South Dakota. Not only do the big birds provide innumerable hunts each year for hundreds of hunters, they are also a favorite of special bird watchers and wildlife fans.

*The author's first northeast South Dakota
Merriam's holds court in her living room.*

CHAPTER SEVEN

FINDING MY "RIGHT STUFF"

It was time to accept a challenge and start calling turkeys by myself. With some help from a friend who knew the landowners and turkey habitat in the area, I had a perfect spot to try my calling effort. A beautiful area bordering Big Stone Lake in Roberts County held a small population of Rio Grande turkeys. I didn't know it at the time, but Roberts County was an extremely important place for turkeys. So important, in fact, the county would become famous in wild turkey hunting history.

Four turkey subspecies including Merriam's, Eastern, Rio Grande and Osceola, are found in different regions of the United States. When all four are harvested, it's considered a Grand Slam by turkey hunters.

Rio Grande was the first subspecies inhabiting northeast South Dakota, followed by Merriam's when they were transplanted in the 1960s. Due to the introduction of Eastern birds in the 1990s, three subspecies could simultaneously be found in Roberts County. Hence, three-fourths of a Grand Slam were found in the same county, or state for that matter, where a hunter could harvest three birds of the "big four."

Hybridization soon took place and the great majority of today's birds consist of traits of all three subspecies. Therefore, no more "almost acquired" Grand Slams are possible in Roberts County.

Back in 1990, the pasture/gulch where I called in my first bird was populated with Rio Grande birds. I had already put a Merriam's on my Grand Slam list, so I was excited on several fronts. My hunting buddy had scouted for me, knew the lay of the land and figured what the birds would do and where they would go. I followed his direction and nestled in by a tree in a ditch on the far end of the gulch.

I scratched out a few yelps, as well as I could. Lo and behold, I heard some gobbles echo through the woods. Turkeys! Hens joined in and before I knew it, the cacophony of gobbles and yelps was coming closer. I couldn't believe it! I actually was calling and the birds were answering. Elated, my self esteem went through the ceiling. I was thrilled.

There was a small ridge eight feet high on the left side of the ditch and then it slanted down to my level. Keeping my yelping going, one answering yelp suddenly became very loud. I stopped calling, not knowing what would happen and I didn't want to get caught moving.

Soon, a hen peeked over the ridge, checking things out for the flock as she stared at me. Time stood still and I swear I quit breathing as I watched her, at 30 yards, walk down the ditch to my level. She continued to yelp and the flock, including the gobbler, continued to answer her.

To my astonishment, my "live" decoy was working for me. A tom's excited gobble became ever closer and my heart beat faster. When he finally poked his red head over the ridge, I almost passed out.

He liked both "hens." Dancing and strutting around the lady with feathers, he was a perfect target. I don't remember taking the shot but the first bird I called in by myself suddenly hit the ground. Now, I was a real turkey hunter and had half of my Grand Slam.

Because I enjoyed being in the gulch, I continued to hunt the same area for several years. How wonderful to lie down in the tender new grass among spring flowers and take a nap in the morning sun. I thought I was in heaven.

The landlady was a great person and we had good visits which I looked forward to every spring.

She gave me slips for plants, told me stories of happenings in the area and warmly welcomed me. One spring she had trouble with wild turkeys tearing up her garden after she had planted it. She asked me to help her, and, of course, I couldn't refuse.

I set up in lilac bushes on the garden edge and waited. Giggling to myself, thinking how ridiculous it looked, I waited as long as I could. No self-respecting turkey came into or even near the garden the entire time. But, I tried to help my hostess and she appreciated it.

This special gulch also afforded me a deep emotional religious experience. The plane crash which claimed the life of South Dakota Governor George S. Mickelson was a shock in 1993. In addition to being a great governor, he was my third cousin and I admired him very much. He had reappointed me to the South Dakota Game, Fish and Parks Commission and enjoyed joining us for various outdoor events. He helped me, through my work on the commission, become an avid outdoor person. A commune with nature in the turkey woods seemed like the perfect way to pay tribute to him soon after word of the tragedy. My favorite place at that time was the turkey gulch.

Standing in a beautiful spot beside a big tree, memories and thoughts of gratitude to God for my blessings in the outdoors and to Mickelson ran rampant through me. I was lost in reverie when I felt a presence. It didn't come with a bang. It simply was there, a fleeting feeling of someone standing next to me. It was a feeling that Mickelson's spirit was there with me, bidding me "you are welcome and it was fun" and goodbye. This is the only way I can explain what I felt. The emotional moment disappeared as quickly as it appeared but left me shaken. I will be forever grateful I experienced it. This happening only deepened my love of turkey woods and turkey hunting.

Driving away from the gulch, I spotted a spectacular Merriam's gobbler strutting in the field about 200 yards away. The sun brightened his white tail feathers and made his body glisten. He appeared larger than life as he strutted for his hens. What a gift the sight was for such an extremely special day, never to be forgotten.

*Wall decoration includes fan
and beard from Black Hills Merriam's
and wings from the northeast South Dakota
Rio Grande shot in the author's special gulch.*

CHAPTER EIGHT

WAS SHE
OR WASN'T SHE?

Big Stone Lake was well known as a good fishing lake. During spring turkey season, walleyes are hungry. Friends invited me to fish and I promised them I'd meet them at noon sharp as I'd be surely finished hunting by then. Wrong.

Mid-morning in the special gulch near Big Stone, gobbles reverberated from the far end of the property. Calling, stopping, calling and not moving, whatever I did was to no avail. The calls did not touch the gobbler's sensibilities. He gobbled but would not move. I'd shut up and he would shut up. I'd yelp, he'd gobble, but never come any closer. Against my best judgment, I moved closer to him.

It's said if a caller moves closer to a gobbling tom, the tom then thinks the hen will come to him (the way it really works in nature). The hunter changing to a closer location usually makes the tom stand his ground and wait, and this he did.

It would soon be noon and I had to meet my fishing buddies. But, I couldn't leave a "hot" tom in the woods. I tried my darndest to get him to move, but he wouldn't. Frustrated and concerned my friends would become worried about me, I had to end this predicament, one way or the other.

I quietly moved from place to place, ever becoming closer to the tom. Peeking around bushes, I could hear him gobbling on the other side of a small hill in front of me. Sitting and waiting and listening to maddening gobbles which never became closer, I began to think my friends had recorded gobbles and were playing a prank on me.

Finally, decision time. In the hot noon sun, slowly Army-crawling up the hill with my shotgun at the ready, it was nerve-racking knowing I had to shoot as soon as I reached the top, but shoot safely. My eyes peeked over the top as I brought the gun up. I was shocked.

The "gobbler" had a blue head and no beard. Dumb-founded, I froze, not believing my eyes. Was this a gobbler? Was this a gobbling hen? What in the heck was it?

Well, "it" didn't stick around long enough for an answer. The bird quickly turned and ran, leaving me on top of the hill wondering what I had just seen.

So much for the "prank" my buddies pulled.

CHAPTER NINE

WILD TURKEYS: NO NORM

You think wild turkeys constantly exhibit the same behavior? Of course not. They change behavior just to make hunting more difficult and make hunters swear. I was told they never jump fences. When hunting the bottom of a gulch near Big Stone Lake, I heard gobbling above me. I decided to give it a try, even though there was a fence on the edge of the small ridge above.

Sure enough, a gobbler approached, liked what he heard and pranced around on the other side of the fence. Not wanting to fly over or crawl under the fence, he weighed his options as hens clucked to his left.

Taking the easy way to some fun, he left to join the hens. Soon, all was quiet. Breeding time. Patiently waiting, I relaxed and imagined the scene, hoping he'd not wear himself out so he'd come back to me.

I finally heard leaves rustling on the ridge, and there he was. I resumed calling with soft purrs and yelps. He paced back and forth, paced and paced some more, but he just couldn't take it.

With one big leap, he jumped over the fence and landed up in front of me. I pulled the trigger and he became a dark-colored ball, rolling down the hill, landing in my lap.

Never try to outguess those birds because they will surprise you every time.

CHAPTER TEN

HAUNTED CANYON?

Ol' Uncle Don and I shared many turkey adventures and our most freaky adventure involved a hunt north of Sica Hollow in Roberts County. Sitting on an ant hill in the dark was a funny adventure, but that's another story.

Karen Borgen and her late husband, Art, operated a horse riding enterprise north of the beautiful park and have wild turkeys inhabiting their land and nearby canyon. They were a fun couple and enjoyed hunters. One morning, Ol' Uncle Don and I arrived at zero-dark-thirty and drove up a path adjacent to the hunting land on one side and a deep canyon on the other. We parked the vehicle and then struggled in the dark to get our vests on and gear ready to go. Suddenly, we both froze.

A horrible never-heard-before howling scream came echoing up the canyon walls beside us.

Needless to say, we loaded our shotguns as quickly as possible, shaking. We had no idea what it was. Waiting in silence for a repeat performance, all was silent. We quietly left the vehicle, not ceasing to look over our shoulders as we slowly walked to our set-up spot. A nice tom cooperated with us after fly-down and Ol' Uncle Don made a perfect shot.

Landowners like to visit and so do we. After showing off the tom, we happened to remember the scream we heard and told the Borgens about it. They sneakily smiled, looked at each other, and then Art asked, "Did it make the hair stand up on the back of your neck?"

Quickly nodding yes, he explained. "Oh, that was just our resident cougar."

Our ride home was rather quiet. Arriving home, I checked cougar sounds on the Internet, and sure enough, we had heard one.

When checking with the Borgen's the next year, they described the cougar family. "Now we see a set of big foot prints and two small sets," Karen said. The last time I hunted there, no big cats were around and that was actually a little disappointing.

Good Ol' Uncle Don and our "cougar bird."

CHAPTER ELEVEN

INTRODUCTION TO TURKEY TOYS: DECOYS

My long-time turkey hunting friends urged me to start using turkey decoys. What could be better than an attractive "hen" for a gobbler to actually see as well as hear? "Birds come running in" was all I had to hear.

Outlaw photographic silhouette goose decoys peppered our set-ups during waterfowl hunting and worked well. Outlaw started manufacturing turkey decoys, so, of course, I had to have a set including a hen, jake and gobbler. Usually only using the hen, arriving gobblers hit the dust. After observing how well decoys worked, I was anxious to try new ones as they appeared on the market. My next hen decoy was a rubber-like foldable little lady, who compared to today's decoys, looked a little sick. Her belly split and called for some surgery, but she accomplished her job until she was retired from duty.

Technology constantly improved decoys and today we have incredible look-alike birds we place in the field. Decoy designers and manufacturers are continually inventing better and better outstanding products. They say "turkeys are getting smarter" so we hunters have to purchase new items to have a more successful hunt. Whether it is true or not, hunting with decoys definitely has been more fun and with new products available, strategy is always changing and hunters are always learning.

My most successful, story-producing and table fare-producing decoy has been Pretty Boy. He is a large life-size tom in full strut, featuring a white head. Gobblers' heads turn white immediately before breeding, so with his white head, he brings in other toms on the run as they want a piece of the action. I have had birds actually attack Pretty Boy.

"Lena" has now joined my family of decoys. She is a real full-mounted feathered hen in submissive position. Her magnetic personality is prophetic, subject of a later story.

CHAPTER TWELVE

IOWA
MUZZLELOADER BIRD

A friend I met during an Iowa Governor's Deer Hunt urged me to hunt an Iowa Eastern bird with her the next spring. It didn't take much persuasion. Using a muzzleloader shotgun was a new twist on this hunt so a couple of lessons were involved.

She used a hen decoy similar to my first one, a foam rubber-like facsimile. After a couple previous unsuccessful set-ups, she placed the decoy and we settled in a row of small trees. A very good caller, she enticed a big Eastern in to flirt with the decoy. I took my shot. The bird flew up in the air three feet and came straight down flat as a pancake. We congratulated ourselves and went to pick him up. We were five feet away from him when he jumped up and ran until he disappeared. We checked his path but he was gone for sure, leaving us standing there with puzzled looks and frowns.

Why didn't I shoot again, you ask? I had a muzzleloader shotgun. I had only one shot, thought it was true and never thought about reloading. So much for the "dead" Iowa bird.

My friend showed me different set-ups using her hen, some hilarious. At one point, we both lay on the ground and she placed the hen on top of her head and Army crawled closer to a tom before she started calling. I could only lay there and laugh. Another time, a jake came in and stood right behind me and I didn't know he was there until I could see her silently giggling.

Although no Iowa bird made it back to South Dakota, the trip was unforgettable. Using the muzzleloader shotgun was interesting and I did use it again here in South Dakota. Turkey sizzled on the grill following that hunt.

CHAPTER THIRTEEN

HUNTING TRIBAL LAND

Sisseton-Wahpeton Oyate tribal lands are adja-cent to our home in northeast South Dakota. Those lands contain beautiful country where lakes, coulees, canyons and wildlife abound. When I was informed how much fun turkey hunting was on tribal land, I had to investigate. Alvah Quinn, director of the tribal wildlife division, was my accommodating contact.

He offered to personally show me good turkey habitat. After telling me about a unique coulee, we drove there and as we came up over the last small hill and peered down into the coulee, we were entertained with a surprising show. A strutting lone gobbler was "doing his thing" on the edge of the woods.

As my heart started beating quicker, I accused Alvah of staging that bird and asked him where his "control strings" were. Laughing, he said, "I told you this is a great place."

Yes, it is a wonderful place. Acres of hardwoods, very steep ravines and small meadows perfect for strutting turkeys runs for two miles and ends near my friend's pasture. Deer, all types of birds, waterfowl flying overhead, wood ducks enjoying the streams and turkeys make this place a piece of outdoor heaven. Hunting there many times, I have introduced Ol'Uncle Don, teenagers and my female hunting friends to the glories of this spectacular coulee.

Among all the adventures in the coulee, a creepy instance is unforgettable. I had Will Brzicka, a new teenage hunter, with me at the time. Upon hearing a hen yelping, we set up and proceeded to call. When the woods became quiet, we spied a man in a navy blue pea coat and brown pants. He was quickly walking to our left on the ridge bottom beside a stream in front of us. Not wearing camo, we wondered what he was doing. Was he hunting or simply walking in the woods? Would he try to harm us?

We should have yelled at him, but something held us back. Without camo on, he just didn't look right. The intruder evidently heard our calls and assumed the "birds" he was talking to had moved up the ridge. He suddenly turned and almost ran up the ridge and away from us. We heard two shots and a cacophony of turkey noises which ended the episode.

Hunters are to speak in a normal voice if encountering another hunter and make him/her aware you are there, but something stopped us. Hunting without camo is probably that guy's normal hunting gear, but it unnerved us.

VOYEURS

Wild turkeys are curious, and sometimes, just plain nosey. While hunting alone I decided to take a walk through an off-shoot of a larger coulee, just to see if there were any birds lurking about. Half-way through the area, the need to relieve myself overcame me.

Alone in the woods granted the perfect solution so I proceeded to take care of the personal task. I idly gawked around the woods during the process. Midway through my procedure, I happened to look up in front of me and dang near fell over. Two large jakes were aimlessly observing the event from about 25 yards.

Well, in that predicament, the plumbing just won't shut off because you will it to.

Gauging how close my shotgun was and thinking of the speed with which I'd have to reach, grab the gun and fire a shot all while squatting with my hunting pants down around my ankles took my breath away.

Silently counting to three, I made the move and the shot echoed through the trees. One jake rolled as the other took off in afterburner mode. Before I knew it, the one I hit jumped up and ran off, not stopping with a second shot. When my pants were pulled up and zipped, I grabbed my vest and gun and took off in hot pursuit of the supposedly wounded bird. Spending a lot of time searching for feathers and ultimately him was fruitless. He was gone.

Having a minute to finally stop and think of what just happened made me laugh. Thank heavens turkeys don't carry video cameras and I hope their curiosity was satisfied.

Folks, I can't make up this stuff!

RADIO SHOW BIRDS

At the time, my co-hort, Mike McKafferty, and I hosted an outdoor radio show in Aberdeen, 80 miles from my favorite coulee. Staying at our nearby Pickerel Lake cabin, I figured I could get up at zero-dark-thirty, turkey hunt and still make it back to Aberdeen in time for our show.

Walking only a partial way through the coulee, my watch told me it was time to turn around and head back to my vehicle. When on the very edge of the woods, I heard a yelp. Hitting the ground immediately, I sat in front of a tree and listened to more yelps down the small ridge behind me. I'd call, stop and call again. It didn't sound like the birds were coming any closer. I fought the urge to turn around to see what was down there. Minutes kept ticking away. A couple more calls and the response I received finally sounded closer. I thought I'd have a chance at these birds. Hearing a gobble, my heart started the "gobbler on the way in" beats. Then, the birds would stop talking. I'd look at my watch and then it would start all over again.

The question going through my head was, "if I turn around and look, can I get in position fast enough to shoot the tom successfully and safely?" I stopped calling and waited for their next move. I had five minutes left on my self-imposed deadline, which stretched out further. Finally, this was it. I had to make a move because I had to leave. Slowly, I turned. Two hens and a tom were three feet behind me. We all jumped and they immediately scrambled down the ridge. If I had only waited two more minutes, they all would have been in front of me. I think I probably swore to myself all the way to Aberdeen.

LANDOWNER HUNT

A very nice gentleman farmer lives about a half a mile across from my favorite coulee. He graciously let me park on his land while I hunted. One time when I came back to my vehicle, I spied three gobblers on the edge of the woods, feeding in his field. I stopped to get permission and he stated he wanted to hunt with me. I grabbed the Pretty Boy decoy and we climbed up a rock pile about 300 yards from the birds. They wouldn't come in with just my calls, so I put Pretty Boy over my head and lay on top of the rock pile, continuing to call. The landowner started laughing and I followed suit and we couldn't stop. The birds just stood and looked at me probably asking themselves, "what is that dumb bird doing on top of the rock pile?"

It dawned on me how dangerous this situation was. A non-ethical person with a rifle could pick me off to get "the gobbler." I took Pretty Boy off my head, the birds walked back into the woods and the "heady" hunt was over.

Never attempt to put a decoy on your head. My knees shake whenever I think about this episode and what could have happened. No turkey is worth your life. I don't recommend turkey fans which you hold in front of you or attach to your gun barrel, either. It's just too easy for an unobservant and unethical hunter to take a shot.

A SNEAKY JAKE

One day while parked in the landowner's field, I saw a jake feeding on the edge of the woods. I continued to walk into the woods because I didn't care he was a jake.

After I was into the woods my thoughts went back to the jake, wondering if he would come in if I called. I sat down in front of a tree, was in the process of getting settled and grabbed my calls. I happened to look up and there he stood, in between two trees 10 yards away, watching me. I was shocked, but then thought if he wanted to be my next meal, so be it. I pulled up the shotgun and fired. And missed. Fired again and missed. He never moved. Unbelievable. The message eventually sunk in and he quickly turned and ran. I couldn't believe he watched me walk in the woods and then walked up to me and stood there through two shots. You never know what tricks turkeys will pull on you or when your gun barrel decides to bend.

GOBBLING TRIO

There were always surprises in the big coulee. During an evening hunt, I ditched the decoys and sat on a ridge overlooking a stream. The early evening sun shining through the trees displayed everything in a golden glow. Enjoying the setting and giving thanks for being able to be there, I started calling softly.

Gobbles! Hearing several simultaneous deep-throated gobbles, I stopped calling and waited. The birds came quickly. Three big gobbler heads appeared on the ridge top, 20 yards from me. They came up in a military row, stood in a row, and as if acting on cue from a choir director hidden in a tree, all gobbled at once. I counted out 1, 2 and 3 and imagined my music director arms giving them the cue to gobble. They continued to stand there, gobbling every few seconds, all at once. It was hilarious.

I couldn't shoot as I didn't want to hit more than one. I just sat there, enjoying the concert. What a treat. As nothing seemed to interest them, they sauntered off to my left and marched down a path leading to the stream, gobbling as they left, all in precision. The production danced around in my head for hours and a smile always appears when I remember the adventure.

A DARK WALK

We are all prone to be stubborn at times and Ol'Uncle Don is no different. On a late afternoon hunt in the coulee, we proceeded to the far east side, about a mile from where we had parked. As the sun continued its setting course, I suggested we call it a day and start walking back to the vehicle. A loud "no" reverberated through the woods. Ol' Uncle Don insisted on exploring where we had heard the last gobbles at the end of the coulee. After spending the time and energy to get where we were, he didn't want to leave without finding the roost tree, regardless of not being able to hunt the next day. I grudgingly went along with his wishes and followed him further and further into the woods. It was getting darker by the minute. Unexpectantly, there was a loud flapping of wings and much cackling. Loud whooshes echoed through the trees. Yes, he found the roost tree, all right. They all flew out. If he had planned on hunting the next morning, he had foiled his own plan.

Off to the vehicle we went, with barely enough light to see. He walked ahead of me and periodically turned around and asked where the heck we were. "I know it wasn't this far," he'd repeat and grumble. Panting while cresting a ridge and seeing the vehicle another half mile away, he really got mad. Reminding him I had tried to tell him we had to leave, he kept trudging away, giving me dirty looks. With gopher holes and rocks littering the prairie, it was a tough walk, especially in the dark. Silence encompassed us as we finally reached the vehicle and also on the way home. The only utterance I made was the final statement, "always trust your guide and act accordingly." He didn't like that, either.

CHAPTER FOURTEEN

SICA HOLLOW

Sica Hollow State Park is a magical place within the Coteau des Prairies, a high plateau approximately 200 miles in length. The Coteau, with its canyons, forested coulees and lakes, rises from prairie flatlands in extreme northeastern South Dakota and continues down through the state to Nebraska. Sica Hollow is nestled on the Roberts/Marshall County line on the Coteau. American Indian folk lore abounds in Sica Hollow. At some times of the year, its streams emit a swamp gas. Hence, the Lakota Sioux culture believes spirits reside in the coulee. The walking trail through the coulee is named Trail of the Spirits. A turkey population is sprinkled throughout the coulee, although they usually like to hang out in the meadows up on top of the Coteau's ridge. It's a wonderful place to hunt. It just takes some work to climb up the steep hillsides to get there.

My young friend, Will Brzicka, wanted to explore the top meadow and see if there were birds up there, so huffing and puffing, we crawled to the top. Two hens greeted us as we poked our heads over the top of the ridge, a good sign there may be gobblers up there. We proceeded to walk and call and set up a couple of times. After resounding gobbles echoed over the meadow, we rushed to an appropriate tree, placed the decoy and started calling.

Soon, a nice Merriam's gobbler decided to check us out. His curiosity got the best of him and Will's shot connected. It was a classic text book hunt because everything happened as planned. A week later to the day, I worked my way up to the meadow by myself. Starting the same procedure as previously, I heard gobbles coming from the identical place where Will killed his bird. However, these birds acted differently and none came walking in as before.

Knowing a hunter is not supposed to move in on a hen, I did it anyway. The theory is a gobbler will mistakenly think a hen is coming to him, not the other way around, and he will hang up (not come in). Changing calls, I tried to sound differently than earlier. The trick worked. A group of birds moved out of the tall grass toward me, only with one surprising difference. These birds were Easterns. One tom couldn't control himself and moseyed over to me, his mistake.

How unique. Carrying two birds out of the same place, seven days apart, one Merriam's and one Eastern. I left the meadow with a grin, remembering again the day on the Coteau when we opened the National Wild Turkey Federation live turkey boxes and became part of the Eastern wild turkey transplant project.

What a wonderful way nature thanked me and all the other conservationists interested in furthering turkey numbers and hunters.

Will Brzicka and his Sica Hollow gobbler.

CHAPTER FIFTEEN

RIM ROCK ROMEO

The hairs stood up on the back of my neck when I heard the gobble.

Lori Goldade and Lila Antonides did exactly as I directed and within seconds were ready to draw a bead on the Merriam's turkey we heard gobble not more than 100 yards from us. Set up behind the women, I waited a few minutes before I started calling.

This was truly exciting as it was the female hunters' first trip to the Black Hills for spring turkey hunting. This was during my early turkey hunting years and I truly wanted to impress upon Lori and Lila how much fun and how exciting turkey hunting really is so we could continue hunting together. Up in Spearfish Canyon, we hoped we would at least hear some gobbles or get a shot at a bird or two. Wanting to successfully call for my good friends, I nervously started started with some soft yelps.

One yelp and the gobbler sounded off again. He was closer. A couple more yelps and a cluck and then it was waiting time. He had answered me every time so I assumed he had fallen in love with me and would come running into our laps giving the gals their first "raw, in the wild, wild turkey show" and a chance to shoot.

A new sound came from my left. Darn. It was a hen. She was yelping, cutting and coming in to me. Hardly breathing, I prayed the gobbler was with her, but, no. He stayed out in front of us, still gobbling but not moving within gun range. The hen poked around, trying to find the "other woman" and bring her back to the gobbler. Since she found nothing but me, she wandered away, back to the tom, telling him in their language she had seen nothing.

He was still gobbling as I used different calls to get his attention, but he wouldn't listen and was walking further away from us. I used all the tricks in my arsenal, but to no avail. The hen had won. He was leaving with her, thumbing his nose at us.

How dare he? He was so close and hot to trot. What happened? We were shocked and couldn't believe he didn't show up as we listened to the echo of his gobbles as he walked down the ridge away from us. Angry thoughts about "Rim Rock Romeo" rolled around in my head. This had been my chance to prove to my friends that I knew what I was doing and could get a turkey in for them. Now he made a fool of me. "Wait until tomorrow, guy, it's gonna happen," I vowed.

With my wavering self-confidence, I worried if my calling would be good enough, if the weather would stay nice and if the birds would cooperate. Lori and Lila were good pheasant and deer hunters so I hoped they would understand my predicament and concerns and still be excited about hunting the wily turkey. When I explained how I felt and maybe I should call a male friend to guide us, they looked at each other and said, "We do not want a man to guide us. We want you. This is a women's hunt and we will be fine."

As I shuffled my feet and said, "Aww, shucks," I was thrilled. There is so very much more to hunting than bagging game and they knew that.

We set off again with the attitude of enjoying a new adventure. Friends can surely inspire a person. The self-confidence they gave me as we embarked on our excursion into the wild was needed and appreciated.

The next day, we set up and tried to call a bird numerous times. Lori and Lila sat and waited and waited for a lover boy to show up. Nothing had answered calls and nothing sounded off. All the Rim Rock Romeos had simply disappeared.

We decided to try and find birds in a different area the next day. Since we had no bird roosted, we slept in the last morning, but worked hard when we got to the hunting area. We all called but came up with nothing. It was windy, which makes turkey hunting difficult. After a while, there was also thunder and intermittent showers. We did have some comic relief listening to a gobbler sound off whenever we heard thunder. I guess it just bothered him. It was hilarious but when it started to rain hard, we had to head back to the vehicle because we were parked on a dirt road.

Were we disappointed? You bet. Ready to give up? Never! Did Lori and Lila have fun? "Yes," they assured me. Did they want to come back the next season? Yes. It was the camaraderie, experiencing all this together for the first time, the laughter and the memories and stories of the hunt. THE HUNT was the important factor. They knew that their first time out.

Lori, Lila and I continued to hunt together for a few years and those early years set the tone for me to this day. Of course, it's great to haul a trophy gobbler out of the woods and then enjoy the special dinner. But, that doesn't happen every time. And, many times, the hunts where no one shot any game are more memorable than when you bring home a tasty meal. Hunting critters in God's wonderful world is truly a blessing and bringing home game is just a bonus.

*Lila Antonides' first Roberts County
Merriam's gobbler.*

CHAPTER SIXTEEN

HUNTING
BIGFOOT COUNTRY

South Dakota is divided by the Missouri River, north to south in the middle of the state. Common terms to identify the two main areas are "East River" and "West River." East River is defined by mostly agricultural land/farms and West River by prairies/ranches. Hunting methods are basically the same, but terrain dictates the specific type of hunting.

It's fun to hunt in different areas and the habitat around Little Eagle, West River, was just that. Huge stretches of prairie meet Grand River breaks west of the village, creating good habitat for turkeys. A friend and I had been to Little Eagle in the 1970's during they hey-day of Bigfoot sightings and I was anxious to visit it again for a turkey hunt.

During the 1970's, the Alexander family ran the Trading Post in Little Eagle and a visit with them was awesome. It was fun to listen to their stories about how their two sons were riding horses in the surrounding woods and came back at a fast gallop, their faces stark white with fright. They told their mother they had seen this huge creature. Their mother knew the boys had seen SOMETHING as frightened as they were.

She showed us dark brown hair caught in neighboring trees. Her husband had brought it home. She also showed us a plaster cast of a huge footprint. Most weird was the recorded scream the creature supposedly made. National television networks were on site, as were media from around the globe at the time. She told fascinating stories about other "paranormal and UFO" happenings around the Little Eagle around the same timeframe.

Mr. Alexander raised St. Bernard dogs and the kennel was beside the house. Bigfoot supposedly ran beside the kennel and terrified the dogs. I fell in love with a six-month old pup who later became our "Brandy" and much loved pet. She was famous as she had been in TV clips on ABC, CBS and NBC news shows. We wished she could've talked.

Fast-forwarding to the turkey hunt, I was reminded of the Bigfoot adventure while approaching Little Eagle. I was anxious to see the area again and secretly wished Bigfoot would run across our path so we could see him.

My good friends, Arnie and Lori Goldade, were with me and we all were excited about this turkey hunt in supposedly "wild" country. Although Lori had turkey hunted with me previously, Arnie had never experienced a wild turkey hunt. He was anxious to know what the lure of spring wild turkey hunting was and we were hoping all would go well for him and he'd take a bird home.

The first morning of the hunt was a bust. Arriving too late, but yet not light, we set up too near the unknown site of a roost tree. Par for the course, the birds' procedure was to fly down and run in the opposite direction.

Scoping out the territory in the light of day, we saw river flats immediately abutted a sharp cliff. Trees on the bottom land were so tall the tops hung over the cliff top, making a perfect place for roosting turkeys. We know turkeys are not dumb and morning fly down chances were 50/50 the birds would come our way. As Murphy's Law states, we again incorrectly chose our spot—on the bottoms. Fly down took all the birds to the cliff and away they went. Of course, a tom or two wouldn't fly down to the bottom for a single hen when he had 20 of them with him.

We sat there anyway, just in case a bird would circle back. Seated 30 yards behind Arnie and Lori, I proceeded to call. Lo and behold, a lone tom sashayed in, but hung up just beyond shooting range. He was on the way to investigate closer when suddenly a deer snorted right behind me. He startled me and my jumping a few inches was all it took for the tom to change his mind and run.

We tried to be smarter the next morning and set up closer to the roost tree. My hunters were in front of me again, hoping for Arnie to have a shot. After paying our dues for some time, a lone tom again came close, but still not close enough. Following some very aggressive calling, the tom stepped within 20 yards of the hunter. Anticipating a shot, I was disappointed when it never came. Regrettably, Arnie never saw the bird in the tall grass.

Although we took no meat or feathers home, my good friends and I still had a great time hunting in "new country."

Even though Bigfoot did not appear for us, it was fun hunting country he supposedly inhabited. The last time I checked with the Alexander family, they told me Bigfoot was "still around." He maybe had a family because small footprints had been seen around a running well. As the story goes, Native Americans see Bigfoot occasionally but were so upset about all the fuss and media frenzy on their sacred land in the 1970's, they and neighboring people tell no one what they see or suspect. What a secret! I wonder if Bigfoot liked wild turkey meat.

CHAPTER SEVENTEEN

FIRST MISS

Parked on a high hill above the Whetstone Valley in northeast South Dakota, it seemed I could see forever. Turning from the outstanding scenery laid out before me and looking at the tree-lined edge of Crawford Coulee, a dark spot caught my attention. Yup, it was a turkey.

After watching him milling around in the grass in the field leading to the coulee, I gathered my gear and slowly walked toward him. He was 250 or so yards from me. He watched me, then meandered back into the trees. I didn't see a beard on him and he never strutted so I figured he was a jake. He disappeared and I kept walking, forgetting about him.

When I reached the trees, I decided to have a first setup near the edge, just to hear if there was anything around. I fooled around and took my time finding a good tree, laid my stuff down and just as I was ready to sit down, I looked up for some reason. There he was--the big jake standing just 20 yards from me, between two small trees. He did nothing but look. We had a stare-down, but I finally thought, "if he is that dumb to stand there and watch me, then he deserves to be in the freezer."

Standing, I picked up my trusty Remington 1187 12-gauge, aimed and let fly. Nothing. He still stood there. I couldn't believe my eyes so I shot again. Nothing except a jerky head twitch. Unbelievable. I fired a third shot at which he simply turned around and sauntered down the hill.

I was mad, embarrassed, couldn't understand the situation and stood in silence as the shot echoed through the trees. This was the first time I have ever missed a turkey. How did it happen? I have been with a few people who have missed and I just didn't understand how a large target like a turkey could be missed. But, now I did it myself. I wasn't used to shooting a turkey from a standing position and I must have shot over his head. It was goofy, whatever it was. And, it was the first and only miss I ever had with my beloved 1187.

A few years later I purchased a lighter shotgun. The 1187 had just "grown too heavy in the closet." I did miss a few times with the new gun and my love of the 1187 shotgun will never be replaced.

Now, I'm not so judgmental about hunters who miss big birds. One point was proven—a person never stops learning, growing or improving.

CHAPTER EIGHTEEN

THE JIM ZUMBO HUNT

Professional hunter and outdoor communicator Jim Zumbo and I became friends at a national Rocky Mountain Elk Foundation annual convention. Little did I know he would later write the Foreward for my book, *Woman's Guide to Hunting.* He knew my passion was turkey hunting so invited me to hunt with him and his friend in the beautiful Black Hills of South Dakota and Wyoming. Sitting on the border of both states, a hunter could theoretically shoot two gobblers at once, one on each side of the border.

Driving, walking, stalking and calling, we three hunted hard for two days, but there were no birds in the bag. The last morning our luck changed. While driving from one spot to another, we spied a bird on a hillside. We stopped up the road, quickly and silently walked to a promising spot below him and set up. We sat in strategic spots so we would all have a chance to shoot. Our guest sat in the closest position, I sat further back and Jim was behind me. Jim proceeded to call and captured the tom's attention.

It didn't take long and the bird was gobbling while he sauntered down the hill. He finally came into view and with a few more hen calls, Jim coaxed him on his way to us. He was a huge Merriam's and a sight to see as he danced around in front of us, offering a splendid show.

This hunt was a big lesson in politeness. Whenever hosting non-resident hunters, the proper etiquette is letting the guest have the first shot. Hardly containing myself with my shotgun ready, it was difficult to wait to shoot. Time dragged on and on as I waited for our friend to take his shot—an easy 20 yards. My trigger finger itched and I could hardly breathe. "Come on, come on," I kept repeating to myself. The tom wouldn't stay there forever. Still, there was no shot.

I didn't know what the problem was so I was ready to pull my trigger when the bird saw something, spooked and ran to my right and out of sight behind the hill. He stopped and gobbled but didn't move back in to us. Out of the corner of my eye, I spied Jim on his haunches slowly walking up to my right and calling, hoping the bird would come back down in front of us in a little different spot.

The gobbler did decide to check us out again, but it only lasted a micro-second. At the same instant

I spotted the bird's red head coming to Jim through the tall grass, Jim also saw him and took a sharp nose dive into adjacent juniper bushes. The bird watched the antic and took off on the run. I was laughing so hard I was shaking and would've scared the bird anyway, had he come closer.

Finally admitting the bird was long gone and after catching our breaths, we stood up, still laughing. The first thing Jim asked was, "Why in the world didn't you guys shoot?"

Our friend's reply was, "I didn't think he was close enough." Grrrrr. Asked why I hadn't shot, I explained again about the guest taking the first shot, then realized I certainly should have if the guest did not shoot in the first few seconds.

We had a great time in beautiful country, saw birds and had our chances. But, I learned a lesson: be too polite and you'll miss your chance to harvest a bird. Now, if a shot isn't taken immediately, it is my turn. To heck with politeness when turkey hunting.

CHAPTER NINETEEN

HUNTING IN MISSOURI

Hunting in new places is always intriguing and fun. Missouri has the reputation of being a fantastic spring wild turkey hunting mecca. Wanting a new adventure involving turkeys, my friend, Robin Matushin, and I made several trips to hunt in southwest Missouri and it was always a great time, whether we brought home feathers or not. One of those times, Robin's daughter, Dr. Elycia Matushin and my friend, Janet Coyne, accompanied us.

The Association of Great Lakes Outdoor Writers hosted an event near Branson which allowed me to meet some great people including turkey hunting outfitters who generously hosted several writers on turkey hunts. Accepting their offer to come back down the next spring on our own to hunt, three of us women made the trip.

Missouri birds are not called "longbeards" as a joke. Missouri Easterns are known for their long 12-inch-plus beards, making them very special. We looked forward to acquiring another notch in our guns.

Staying at the outfitter's rustic lodge in the middle of turkey country was, indeed, a blast. Everyone we met at camp was great and we had fun sharing turkey stories over some ultra-delicious camp cooking.

We had to work for our birds as we didn't just walk out the door and shoot them. Walking and setting up a blind and calling was a proven method and simply sitting in the woods by a tree was another. Two of us women were successful, but it took over two days to pull the triggers.

*Missouri Eastern birds are known as
"longbeards" and rightly so as the author's
gobbler's beard measured 12.5 inches.*

Before our second trip to Missouri, a new shotgun had joined my arsenal, a Benelli Model M2 12-gauge semi-automatic. Having not connected with a bird in South Dakota that particular spring, I was anxious to get a Missouri bird.

Sitting on the ground, not in a blind, had always been my method of operation since I started turkey hunting. My Missouri guide, Eric, insisted we take his Double Bull blind and set it up. My first mistake was missing a bird at 15 yards. I blamed it on never hunting/shooting turkeys from a blind before. To his chagrin, I also missed two more chances. The most disappointing sound to hear when hunting is the trigger simply going "click" when the target is in position. The trigger stubbornly staying stationary at the perfect time can throw a monkey wrench into the hunt. After missing the third time, we gave up for the day, closely inspected the shotgun and hit the shooting range.

I don't remember ever being so angry, disappointed and having no possession of confidence. When Eric used my gun for the first shot at the range, his aim was true. So, the problem was ME. However, the gun was also at fault. I discovered when putting a shell in the chamber, the action had to be forcefully closed or the gun would not fire. I had not known that. It had never happened with my Remington 1187. Making certain the action was properly closed involved letting it slide itself closed, no matter how much noise it made and pushing on it to insure it was correctly closed.

The second problem involved me having to aim a little differently while hunting in a blind. The outfitter kidded me about the "barrel being bent," and he said I would not be allowed in camp the next year if I brought that gun. I went home from that hunt feeling badly, but still had a good time with friends, especially stopping in Branson, Missouri's music city, and catching a few shows on the way home.

I took the same shotgun the next season, but knew all its quirks by then. However, that year, the birds did not cooperate. We couldn't figure out why they always came in from the sides and never walked in front where the decoy was. Their pattern demanded I turn around in the blind and they seemed to hear or see me and left in a huff. Finally, the last day, three gobblers marched in from my right, walking and gobbling in front of us. Yes! The shot connected and a Missouri bird was mine.

My friends were successful, too, and it was great to have feathers accompanying us home. The last year in Missouri was tough hunting as the weather just did not cooperate. We went home empty-handed but still had lots of fun memories.

It was good to prove to myself I could still hit something. I had more confidence later when I used HEVI-SHOT, thanks to Janet Coyne who said I "must use those shells." I'll always be grateful to her for insisting I use them. Winchester Elite turkey loads or the equivalent are also high on my list.

Following the Missouri hunt, Janet and her daughter, Krista, and I hunted northeast South Dakota and the hunt was classic with Janet downing a nice gobbler at 20 yards.

Robin Matushin and her daughter,
Elycia Matushin, and their Missouri longbeards.

*The Missouri turkey hunting trip included
a side trip to beautiful Bennett Spring State Park
to have fun fishing for trout. Left to right,
Janet Coyne, the author, Robin
and Elycia Matushin.*

CHAPTER TWENTY

A BEATEN UP TOM

Archery hunting was all he talked about. After two years of shotgun hunting, my young friend, Will Brzica, wanted more. Shooting a spring tom with a bow was on his list for a new experience. He was very good at scouting and had found a promising spot near Pickerel Lake. Will discovered turkeys loved to roost in the area and he wanted to try archery hunting there.

His Double Bull Blind was perfect with its black interior and we set it up a fair distance from the roost trees, beside a clump of small trees.

Gobbles from the roost echoed over the prairie, music to our ears. When the hens started their morning ritual, our hearts beat just a little faster. Shortly, the birds flew down. Milling around, yelping and gobbling, they seemed to march in circles until they decided in which direction to go. Luckily, it was ours.

Will and I made plenty of noise together and obviously sounded inviting as the birds started moving our way. A nice group of 25-30 turkeys looked promising. We made certain we were positioned correctly, shutting the "windows" on the proper side of the blind and made room for Will to move the bow. I peeked through the slit beside the window and kept track of the flock.

It was fun for me, simply calling and watching, not worrying about shooting. However, the closer they came, the more my adrenalin kicked in. They were bound determined to get to wherever the turkey sounds were coming from.

Three gobblers briskly walked up to my side of the blind, then slowed down when they were right beside me. My breath caught in my throat as they brushed their feathers against my corner of the blind. I could have touched them. An Eastern led the way, followed by a Merriam's and another Eastern. (This was before they were hybridized). I guess I expected the usual gunshot, so when all I heard was "swish" and a tom lay on the grass, it felt like "what happened?" This was the first time I had experienced bow hunting and wasn't prepared for the quietness of the kill. It certainly surprised me—one little noise and a big tom was down. But that wasn't the end of the show.

The birds had continued on past us going up a small knoll. Suddenly, the two other toms turned and looked at the dead bird. They must have looked at each other and simultaneously said, "let's go" and ran back and beat up the dead gobbler. They kicked, pecked and jumped on him, would run up the hill, then run back down and do it all over again. They delivered this beating three or four times. It was hilarious—they wouldn't quit until Will moved out of the blind.

The hunt was over, but what another exciting experience in the quiet of a beautiful spring morning.

Will Brzicka and his first archery spring gobbler.

CHAPTER
TWENTY-ONE

TRICKERY

They always say, "There's more than one way to skin a cat." It's true for spring turkey hunting, too.

Robin Matushin, Christi Johnson and I spied a good-sized flock of birds, including a few nice gobblers, in a quiet farmyard east of Pickerel Lake. Following the procedure of finding the landowner and asking permission did not pan out well. The farm was unoccupied and the owner was in absentia. Upon contact with the owner's granddaughter, permission was not granted. On to Plan B.

The huge acreage across the road from the lonesome farm was planted to CRP, (Conservation Reserve Program). CRP fields are planted to good quality grasses for conservation purposes and are not actively farmed or tilled. CRP acres are also good for wildlife. The field was a Walk-In-Area, meaning public hunting was allowed. Nurturing an idea I had, I kept it to myself for the time being.

We took a drive down the lonesome farm road again in the afternoon. No birds were in the yard, but there were three gobblers in the field just south of the farm. Time to unveil my devious plan.

We would hunt the same turkeys, alright, but from across the road. Pretty Boy decoy would be placed on a small rise adjacent to an approach in the field. We would lay in the grass and try to call the gobblers to us. The three guys gave us a show, but wouldn't move from their spot in the field about 200 yards from us. Not one call in my vest would budge those stubborn birds. Giving up, we sat up in the grass and began talking strategy and joking around, not paying attention to anything but the three birds in the field.

Suddenly, Christi sat up straighter, looked to her right and asked, "What's that thing on the road?" There seemed to be a huge black medicine ball or big tire rumbling up the road to us. "Turkey!" I yelled and "get down." For novice hunters, "get down" means keep your head down, too, and that is what Christi did. Robin and I carefully monitored the action by peeking through the tall grass. The big black ball picked up steam as it ran up the middle of the road. The bird had spied Pretty Boy and nothing was going to stop him from a good fight.

Seeing he was not going to stop, we told Christi to get ready. As the bird ran closer, Christi was hurriedly whispering through the grass, "I can't see him! I can't see him!" We yelled "Shoot!" over and over and nothing happened as the creature was almost upon the decoy.

With us screaming "Shoot!" Christi's head appeared above the grass and her gun finally fired, catching the tom in mid-air as he flew up in afterburner mode to attack Pretty Boy. What a sight! He folded at Pretty Boy's "feet."

That tom was a half a mile away when we first saw him on the road and he never slowed down or wavered as he raced to fight Pretty Boy. Incredible. And then, to be shot in mid-air attack mode!

It's situations like this which make the blood run, heart pound, adrenalin flow and instill hunters with fodder for a lifetime of stories, memories and friendships.

Yup, there really is more than one way to skin a cat—or turkey.

The author and Christi Johnson with her gobbler via "turkey trickery." Luckily, Pretty Boy survived the hunt to work another day.

CHAPTER TWENTY-TWO

BIG BOB

My friend, Christi Johnson, brought her non-tur-key-hunting husband, Ross, along turkey hunting so he could taste the experience.

While driving to a previously good spot in a tree claim, we spied birds across the road. Quickly parking and then walking to where they were likely to come across, we placed Christi's husband deep under a cedar tree, pulled branches down around him and we all sat down. There was a small rise in front of us, allowing a perfect shot for when a bird would show himself. No need to for a decoy. My box call scraped out a couple yelps.

Gobbles immediately resounded over the prairie and Christi held the gun tighter as the birds were on their way to us. We heard some gobbles to the left, some to the right, then it was quiet for a bit.

Shocking us, this huge "thing" that resembled a gobbler jumped up over the rise and ran straight at us.

He did not stop. He did not slow down. He was scary-looking as his head was humongous. He stampeded right to us. He looked like a mutant. Christi finally found her wits about her and fired a shot. Down he went and never moved.

Slowly, we made our way to him, anxious to see this oddity of nature. He was a mature gobbler, all right, with the largest head I have ever seen. It was weird.

As Christi's husband crawled out from under the cedar tree, he was yelling, "What's the matter with him?"

Christi named him "Big Bob" but "Alien Bird" also fit.

CHAPTER TWENTY-THREE

BLIZZARD HUNT

Blowing snow and low visibilities usually mean goose and duck hunting during the waterfowl season, but blizzard conditions also make fall turkey hunting interesting. My friend, Christi Johnson and her husband, Ross, again are at the center of the story. Weekends were the only time Christi could hunt and weather never stopped her. She and Ross would have to drive 70 miles, straight into bad weather, but they still wanted to hunt this particular day. I was glad I only had to drive five miles.

Laughing when we drove into his farmyard, my farmer friend, Harvey Opitz, said, "Have at it," as he retreated into the warm house in the storm. It was late afternoon, the time when birds came into the feedlot to peck around for feed. We had to dress to fit the weather. Ross wore a white camo suit and Christi and I hunkered down under white sheets.

We chose to sit at the corner of a nearby shed, on a ready-made bare spot on the backside of a snowdrift. We thought we could safely watch by poking our heads up just a bit above the snow, holding the sheets over our heads.

Although we were careful to stay hidden, we thought we had it made with all the blowing snow. Wrong. The first birds ran into the lot, screeched to a halt, turned and skedaddled back out. It was amazing they could still see us. Experiencing moments like this reminds me of the fantastic eyesight God gave wild turkeys. We played it even more careful, but to no avail. They always seemed to spy our heads poking up over the snowbank.

It was decision time as the situation was not working. The farm house was nearby so we stealthily moved into the garage, left the door open a crack and took turns peeking our disguised-in-white heads out the crack to monitor the birds. We listened and carefully watched the feedlot. The birds would still be in shooting range if they came back. And, come back they did.

A tom was on the way into shooting range. I slowly backed away from the door, telling Christi to step up, open it further and then shoot. All worked as planned. Birds were chomping feed and never noticed the door opening. Christi stepped up, raised the shotgun, pulled the trigger and....nothing. Nothing at all. She couldn't pull the trigger. It was full of snow and totally frozen tight. In the excitement and confusion of all the blowing snow and moving to the garage, none of us thought to have a "trigger check." After a few blue words and watching the turkeys fly out of the feedlot yet again, we slammed the door shut and hung our heads. Just then, one of the two garage doors made a noise. Melanie, Harvey's wife, was coming home. Now, we were in a worse predicament.

We had to quickly make a decision. Do we, the "three white ghosts," jump out at her and scare her as she comes into the garage and maybe take a chance she'll panic and drive through the opposite wall? Or do we simply line up against the nearest wall, stay quiet and then quietly talk to her as she gets out of the car? Or do we wait until she is completely out and shuts the door, then scare the heck out of her? What if she has breakable things in her arms and she panics and drops them? We had no time for a meeting. She had stopped the car and hadn't seen us.

We quietly stood by the wall and waited until she slammed the car door shut, knowing what was coming wasn't going to be good no matter how it played out. Our hearts were pounding so hard, not from seeing turkeys, but in anticipation of her reaction. I quietly said, "Hi, Melanie." She looked over to us with a surprised look on her face, but no adverse reaction. We were nearly fainting, but she outsmarted us and was fine—like a person runs into three white ghosts in the garage every day.

Surprisingly, we were all invited back to try and score a bird, but advised to try in decent weather. Melanie was still laughing when we left.

CHAPTER TWENTY-FOUR

A MISTAKE WITH DRAKE

Although I taught grandson Drake how to deer hunt, a tradition he carries on today along with waterfowl hunting, my tutelage for spring wild turkey hunting didn't take. We were both excited back when he was a young boy out after his first turkey gobbler. However, it wasn't to be.

Hindered by only being able to hunt weekends because of school, he only had one weekend to chase big birds with me on tribal land. South Dakota's spring weather did not cooperate and neither day was a good "turkey day." Cold, cloudy, windy—the kind of days you want to be inside with a book. But, Drake was a trooper and we were seriously hunting.

Nothing worked for us. We couldn't find birds where they had previously been. We walked and hunted hard, but to no avail. Not ready to give up, we walked down a trail, straining to see a bird. To our surprise, a big-bearded guy was sauntering down a fence line a half mile away from us.

The gobbler spotted us and walked away from us and into some trees. Thinking I could maybe call him in, we quickly made tracks across the field to the end of the trees. Not wanting the bird to get too far, we hurried and got the decoy set up and sat down. The place was not flat. To my dismay, we were in a tiny gully. I placed Drake facing east, the direction from which the bird would probably come. I sat on his left, somewhat behind him, and started yelping with the box call to get the tom's attention.

The tom liked it and answered. I stopped calling as he was coming closer and I was confident Drake would get a shot. Wrong. Just as the gobbler started to answer us, the morning sun peeked out. I didn't think about Drake facing east with his glasses on. He had a mask, but it was on over his nose, not covering his glasses.

We became more excited as the gobbles were very close and before we knew it, the bird came running down through the gully. He broke out of the trees, took one look at Drake and raced up the steep side of the gully and was gone. Drake never got a shot.

I had not counted on the sun coming out while we were sitting there. The reflection off his glasses was just too much for the bird. He knew something wasn't right and left as fast as he could. I still feel badly about this hunt because it was my fault with my grandson. Of all the people I wanted to experience spring turkey hunting, it was Drake. He did learn "it's why it's called hunting and not shooting," though. I am hoping there is still time for us in the spring turkey woods and he will come to fall in love with turkey hunting as much as deer hunting. We need another wild turkey fanatic in the family as I am still the only one.

CHAPTER TWENTY-FIVE

EERIE HUNTING SPOT

My grandson, Drake Halbkat, did want a second chance to bag a bird so we obtained tribal licenses. "Go to the graveyard," we were told. We had been hunting and not having very good luck. We needed a new spot so we followed advice from a tribal member whose home was a true war museum. Fascinating articles and items commanded our attention while we were there visiting and asking permission to hunt in the area.

Our new friend also enchanted us with tribal legends and stories and directed us to walk through his pasture where various tribal activities take place.

"Sit behind a big gravestone and just wait for the turkeys to come," we were told. In the evening before roosting, turkeys left their feeding area at the little farm across a paved road. "They always parade on the driveway, cross the road and walk through the graveyard gate to the trees." It sounded good to us so we thanked the guy and left. Although we couldn't believe it, Drake and I were on the way to the tiny tribal cemetery to hunt our new spot.

Now, if you have never done this, you have to experience the feeling to understand it. It was eerie, rather spooky, somewhat embarrassing and seemed somehow wrong and inappropriate to be there. As cars passed by on the paved road, some people looked, many didn't. We wondered what we looked like to the unfortunate people who happened to spy us. Seeing a big figure and a small figure, covered in camouflage, crouched behind a gravestone with guns must have been a sight.

Did they think we were ghosts? We were waiting to be buried? We were scarecrows? Terrorists? Or even rational hunters? It was rather comical as we wondered what each of us would think when faced with the scene we presented.

We waited and waited—patience being the name of the game in turkey hunting. We never heard anything nor saw anything resembling a turkey. Had we been "duped?" Had it been a joke and I was naïve enough to take my grandson to hunt in a cemetery? Were they driving by laughing at us?

We'll never know. The beginning of twilight found us scurrying back to our vehicle. No way would be chance being caught in the dark in camo in a graveyard!

CHAPTER TWENTY-SIX

AIRBORNE TOMS

The bright green pasture falls from a small farm and forms a triangle surrounded by trees. There is no prettier sight than looking down from the farm or an adjacent ridge and see strutting toms showing their iridescence in the sun. Springs within the trees form a small creek which flows into the pasture. Turkeys have created a super highway beside the creek as they come out from their roost to display in the morning.

My friend, Teresa Bair, was hunting her first spring gobbler. We set up at zero-dark-thirty on an overlooking ridge and because birds have always been plentiful at the site, we were excited for a potential "slam dunk."

Sitting near a fence line in trashy weeds for cover, we patiently waited. We jumped to attention when we heard the first hen on the roost in the trees below and were exhilarated to hear gobbles. While joining in the birds' conversations after the eastern sky turned bright pink, echoes of fly down wings flapping were music to our ears. The angle of their voices told us the birds were on the pasture's edge, making their way to the middle and directly below us where we could not see them. Calling sporadically, two gobblers answered and sounded off particularly loud telling me they were interested in us. We hoped they would come up the side of the ridge and then walk in front of us.

A few minutes later, the two birds were silent. We sat and waited. And waited. And waited. Thinking they had disappeared, we let down our guard and relaxed. Suddenly and simultaneously, the two huge toms flew up over the ridge edge with wings and necks spread out making them look like some kind of small bombers and almost hit us in our faces! I swear one of their heads brushed the end of my gun barrel.

Teresa and I jumped, probably screamed (we don't remember) and lost our breath. The poor toms were just as shocked as we were and ran off in afterburner mode. After thoughts were collected and heartbeats returned to normal, we stood up to start picking up decoys. Another shock was in store.

While setting up the decoys in pitch dark, I thought the site was on the edge of a very gentle slope down to the pasture. Wrong. I had very nearly missed stepping over and dropping down the side of a huge drop-off, or hole, straight down about 20 feet, in the side of the ridge. Two more steps and I would've met my own Waterloo. And that is why the birds flew up the ridge right into us.

Moral: always know exactly what is in front of you when you set up in the dark.

CHAPTER
TWENTY-SEVEN

LUCKY FIRE DISCOVERIES

There can be other experiences happening during fall turkey hunting which simply add to the flavor of being in the outdoors and at the right place at the right time.

A friend and I were hunting close to Pickerel Lake, not expecting much success as the northwest wind was blowing a straight 30 miles per hour. However, we found a small flock of birds on the down side of a hill so we planned a stalk and sneak hunt. My friend's shot was true and she had her first bird.

Photographing the birds is always important and we wanted a good background, so we drove to the Pickerel Lake State Recreation Area on the west side of the lake. After posing for pictures, we were sitting on a picnic table, reliving the hunt when we heard it--a cracking sound in the trees behind us.

We couldn't figure out what it was, so we laughingly made up reasons and joked about them. When she took a glance behind her, she quickly turned completely around, looked up and with a shocked look and said, "There's smoke! There's a fire behind us!"

It was terribly scary because if the fire really got going in the stiff hot wind, the entire east side of the park along with many homes would be destroyed. Not having cell phone service where we were, I grabbed my phone and ran up a small hill to call the park office. No one answered at the office so I tried to call the nearest fire department. The reception was spotty and my call was cutting out. The fire was growing and we were scared to death. Not knowing if the fire department received my message, I had to do something else.

Knowing the people who lived on a small farm across from the park entrance, I drove there. Luckily, the lady had a police scanner and had heard the call. She told me the fire department was on the way, but I called again to make sure.

It seemed to take forever for the firefighters to arrive. We were scared as the fire was increasing every minute. When they finally arrived, they quickly contained the blaze. They checked the origin of the fire and found charcoal briquettes on the ground. Some campers had obviously used the camping spot and instead of leaving their coals in the fire pit, or better yet, completely dousing the fire, they picked up the still-alive charcoal, threw it in the trees and left the park.

Thank heavens for fall turkey hunting. The fire could've been extremely devastating had we not been at the park photographing a turkey.

A few years later, another friend, Teresa Bair, and I were fall turkey hunting, again around Pickerel Lake. Just two miles after we left the house, we attempted a left turn when she said, "Look, there's smoke behind those trees!"

"Those trees" partially hid an abandoned old house. It was a huge two story home with a large fireplace attached to one side. It had been a beauty in its day with a huge open stairway and beautiful oak woodwork and flooring amid other nice amenities. It also featured an interesting history.

The house had been used as a pheasant and waterfowl hunting lodge in the 1940-50s. The "Blue Goose Lodge" hosted many celebrities as hunting guests, including movie actor Clark Gable. It had always been fun to point out the house to our visitors and tell the story while driving by.

The Lodge had always been a special landmark in the area and we were shocked when we drove around the trees and saw it on fire. Smoke was curling out of an upper window. We couldn't believe our eyes. No one was around, in or out of the yard. After calling the fire department, we were disappointed. They said all the nearby fire trucks were fighting other fires at the time and didn't know when they would get there. The dispatcher told me there had been a rash of suspicious fires at the time and asked if we had seen anyone around.

Huge flames started coming out of the top of the house, and still the firetrucks had not shown up. There was a tall pine tree in front of the house and when the fire reached the tree, it exploded in flames. Vehicles sporadically pulled in from the road to watch the fire and I wanted to call the dispatcher again. The house was engulfed with flames and had started a ground fire burning its way to a grain bin and some hay bales. A tree claim was next in line to burn.

Finally, we heard a siren. A small fire truck drove into the yard, all that was available at the time. The county sheriff followed. Shortly, a neighboring farmer brought his tractor and loader and dug dirt around the bales, stopping the flames.

The house collapsed in on itself, leaving only the unique fireplace standing. What a sad ending to a legendary landmark. The exact cause of the fire is still unknown but suspicions point toward an exploding meth lab in the abandoned showplace. The fireplace has since fallen into the debris.

Again, fall turkey hunting does offer interesting experiences not to be forgotten.

CHAPTER TWENTY-EIGHT

OL' UNCLE DON: THE SNORING HUNTER

Here we go with another Ol' Uncle Don adventure and my tipster husband.

While Ol' Uncle Don and I hunted in another spot, my husband, Bruce, was driving around our lake when he spotted gobblers picking around in some baled cornstalks on the end of a field. When Bruce later told us about the birds he'd seen, we decided to set up there the next morning. We called and received permission and we were set.

As usual, morning came quickly. Uncle Don met me on "our corner" and we were on our way. We only had the Pretty Boy decoy for this hunt and the plan seemed very simple. The birds roosted across a small blacktop road in a tree line a half mile away from the field with the cornstalk bales. The bales were just inside the field and the birds were obviously used to feeding there after their morning hormone run. We settled in amongst the bales and waited.

As usually happens, there is time to relax and chill before birds show up. Uncle Don was so relaxed he went to sleep. I was lost in thought until the first gobble echoed over the prairie field. Soon, a cacophony of gobbles became louder, then very loud. Turning my head to take a look, the shocking sight of six big gobblers running across the field and heading our way caused me to lose my breath. Faster and faster they ran to our bales, ready to greet Pretty Boy and not in a nice way.

They were crossing the road and would quickly be upon us, but I had a big problem. Ol' Uncle Don was not only sleeping, he was snoring, and not lightly. Waking a person in a living room or even a bed usually causes them to jump and yell "WHAT?" I was afraid to wake him for fear he'd act true to form and scare the birds before he had a chance to shoot. Thank heavens we were sitting close together because he did not have his hearing aids at the time. He just HAD to wake up. Softly nudging him, snores continued. The birds were getting close and the closer they got, the bigger the chance was of scaring them when he woke up.

Shutting my eyes, I took a deep breath and decided, "this was it." I nudged Uncle Don, hard. To my surprise, he only jumped a little bit and there was no noise. He opened his eyes to the sight of six toms playing ring-around-the-rosy with Pretty Boy, chasing, yelping, squawking and getting ready to gang up on the decoy.

Uncle Don didn't seem to hear my whispered "shoot." I couldn't figure out what he was waiting for so repeated the order. After what seemed long minutes, his gun finally boomed and one gobbler folded. I was a wreck and asked him why he waited so long.

"I was just trying to pick out the biggest one and it took awhile," he responded with a laugh. No one is luckier than him, I swear.

Soon, the elderly landowner drove into the field. After visiting a minute, he did a double take when he looked at Pretty Boy. "Oh, he's a decoy. I wondered why he just stood there."

From then on, Ol' Uncle Don was not allowed to go to sleep, even with his hearing aids in use.

*Ol' Uncle Don woke up in the nick
of time for this beauty.*

CHAPTER TWENTY-NINE

A FALL HUNT

Some turkey hunters told me fall turkey hunting wasn't any fun. Listening to others' fall turkey hunting episodes was like listening to an account of pheasant hunting. In fact, I tried it once and it wasn't any fun, especially compared to spring hunting. While researching true fall turkey hunting methods, I became excited and curious to try it the "real" way.

My young friend, Will Brzicka, had a fall hunting tag which allows hens or toms, so we traveled to a favorite hunting spot, the Borgen ranch again. Karen laughed when we told her what we were going to do.

Our first step was to locate a flock of birds, which was easy. Yelling and running at them to scare them was next, and run they did. They all quickly scattered through the canyon where we had previously heard the mountain lion.

Then it was time to set up on the side of the ridge, this time behind a tree. Will sat behind a large rock beside me. After granting silence for a bit, we proceeded to call. We used some hen yelps, but mostly a kee-kee call, the sound young poults make when trying to find the hens and rejoin their flock.

Our calls were answered. Birds kept getting closer and we became more excited. Shortly, hens and poults were running at us from all directions. They came in from 360 degrees, up the ridge, down the ridge and from the sides. Poor Will didn't know which one to shoot first. A hen (legal game in the fall) walked right up the ridge to him and was a perfect target, but Will somehow got hung up behind the rock and didn't shoot quick enough. She was spooked and ran.

The birds were not completely frightened away from his movement, they just went back down the ridge some and started coming back. Determined to hit the hen this time she came close, Will took the shot. He missed. This time, most of the flock ran completely away. We sat and waited and then started calling again. Lo and behold, the same hen walked in to Will. We couldn't believe it. She was so excited, she didn't quit running and he was even more excited when he took the shot. But again, missed her.

All we could do was laugh. We had been in a situation we'd never experienced before, learned a lot and had a good time in the woods. Yes, fall turkey hunting is definitely different than spring hunting, and it's a lot of fun.

CHAPTER THIRTY

A MOST GENEROUS LANDOWNER/ SPORTSMAN/FRIEND

One of the most important and rewarding bene-fits of hunting is the people you meet. Some of those people will become lifelong friends. I am truly the beneficiary of the kindness of a wonderful couple I met through turkey hunting.

Following a speech I gave for a conservation district banquet where I mentioned turkey hunting and habitat, a South Dakota Roberts' County commissioner approached me.

"I have lots of turkeys on my land and I want to invite you to come and hunt," said Truman Nelson. That was all it took and it was the beginning of a special relationship with Truman and his lovely wife, Nova, on their ranch in the Prairie Coteau Hills.

Truman has a spectacular piece of heaven inhabited by turkeys, deer, coyotes and other wild-life. He has a priceless attachment to his land and he and Nova love wildlife and treat their place as a refuge. When he invites a person to hunt, that hunt is extremely special and usually one-of-a-kind. Whether successful results or not, the experience is always remarkable.

Truman, in addition to all of his other good qualities, is a champion trap shooter. Winning state titles and participating in national shoots across the country are part of his life. His life also includes a great sense of humor. And with turkey hunting, my friends and I have supplied him with much fodder for stories and laughter.

Most notable is the episode of the abandoned blind. At Truman's suggestion, my two friends, Robin Matushin and Christi Johnson, and I set up my 3-D turkey blind in a far corner of his pasture. Turkeys come down from roosts in the adjoining coulee and pasture and amble through this particular corner to feed--a perfect spot, or so we thought.

Arriving one morning at zero-dark-thirty, we set up and waited. And waited. And waited. Nothing. No turkey yelps, no turkey gobbles, nothing. Thoroughly chilled through at 9:00 a.m., visions of Nova's hot coffee swirled through our heads. Losing patience, the need for coffee won. We left the blind in place, walked to the vehicle, drove around the section and into Truman's yard.

Coffee was on the kitchen table immediately. Truman and Nova's kitchen window faces their pastures and far off hills and they get a kick out of watching meandering turkeys stroll through their acres. We were on our third cup of coffee when Truman started laughing as he watched out the window. Wanting to see what had caused the outburst, we rushed over to the window.

Yup, several long-bearded toms were checking our blind. They curiously walked by and then stopped for a good look right beside it. They inflamed my intelligence. How dare they! My buddies ultimately thought it was funny, too. The guide (me) was the only one who didn't think so.

Coffee cups were quickly placed on the counter and we scurried out the door. We stealthily walked to the blind. No bird was in sight. In fact, we stayed there until very late morning and no birds ever did show up. Oh well, Truman had his laugh for the week. So many funny things have happened during hunting at Truman's, he is always anxious for us to come back to supply more entertainment.

*Truman and Nova Nelson are great people,
conservationists and good friends.*

CHAPTER THIRTY-ONE

A LATE FALL DOUBLE

Even when in high school, Dylan Hanson was a one-woman hunting machine. Plenty of waterfowl hunts only made her hunger for more. One day, she surprised me by telling me she would like to turkey hunt. The fact thrilled me because she gave me another reason to spend more time in the turkey woods with a new hunter.

Because of her school activities, she had limited time for turkey hunting the next spring. Not giving up, one day we embarked on a late afternoon hunt. She was introduced to methods and manners of spring hunting, but to no avail. The woods stayed disappointedly quiet and there were no turkeys in sight. So much for spring turkey hunting for Dylan. On the way home, I did remind her of our fall season and her spirits rose.

Summer passed quickly, arrangements were made, a date set and we were off late that fall for another turkey adventure. As fall hunting is completely different than spring hunting, our method was also different. We visited with our landowner friend and paid attention to his remarks about turkey behavior this time of year. There was snow on the ground which made birds very easy to track.

A well-travelled path ran from a pasture gate in front of a cattle loading chute on the farm. Weighing options of where to sit to ambush the birds occupied our thoughts. We decided Dylan should sit immediately beside the chute. I sat right behind her. Whether toms or hens came sauntering by, she was ready.

We sat in silence, waiting and watching. Nothing was moving anywhere. We started talking, sharing hunting stories, shared hunting goals and desires. Reaching for the field glasses, the black blobs 150 yards away proved to be our prey. And, they were headed our way, gobblers, jakes and hens. We sat in pure silence as we peeked through the board slats of the cattle chute, our hearts beating a little faster with each yard the birds covered. I had instructed Dylan on where and how to shoot and was confident she would connect.

It was unbearable to sit still while watching the long string of birds approaching us. I just hoped she remembered what I had told her and didn't jump them too early. I needn't have been concerned.

A few hens led the pack up to 10 yards away from us, and then we spied some big gobblers following. I whispered to Dylan to let the hens go (if they did not spook right away when they saw us on the other side of the chute), and shoot a gobbler when he appeared. I hoped it would work but didn't have time to think about it. The birds were on us before we knew it.

"Boom." Dylan's shot rocked the silence and a gobbler was down in the snow. Hens immediately took off in all directions, one flying over the fence they had just walked through. Dylan turned simultaneously as the gobbler fell. She swung the shotgun at the flying hen, pulled the trigger and another bird hit the snow. This high school girl had a double!

That was some fantastic shooting. She quickly stood up, ran and looked at the gobbler and then ran to the hen. I'll never forget her beaming face as she walked back to me carrying the hen and then stepping over to pick up the gobbler. When Dylan does something, she gets it right.

Her face was not the only one beaming. It was so fun to first talk about the hunt, plan it for sure, take our places by the chute and anticipate scenarios about what the birds would do and how they would perform, and then to have her shoot a double. I was extremely proud of her. So were her father and grandfather when we arrived back at Dylan's farm. I had Dylan pose with her birds outside a shed and then told the guys to come out and look. Two more beaming faces appeared immediately.

Dylan Hanson and her lucky fall double.

CHAPTER THIRTY-TWO

A PICKEREL LAKE CLASSIC

Coyotes start their late evening howling immedi-ately preceding sunset, the same time walleyes start biting during ice fishing on Pickerel Lake. It was always fun to hear my "friends" and know all was well in the wildlife world. With coyotes, deer, rabbits, fox and other critters, we have had plenty of wildlife to enjoy in our 37 years living on the lake. To my delight a few years ago, another treat was in store.

The first turkey gobble which echoed across the lake was like a lightning strike. My head flew up, my ears perked up and breathing stopped. A sense of wonder enveloped me. A wild turkey! At the time, they populated an area northeast of us so it was at least a 10-mile drive to observe or hunt them. There had been none in the immediate lake area, until I heard the explosive gobble. It was "music to my ears."

Procreation of the earlier transplant of Easterns sub species in northeast South Dakota was successful and provided a large increase in all turkey populations. Birds meandered into areas not previously populated. It was very exciting to hear birds at the lake, joining the menagerie of other wildlife. Naturally, the next logical step was "Hmmmm, wild turkey hunting in my own immediate area, right where I live."

Pickerel Lake is long and narrow and all sounds echo back and forth across the water. Turkey gobbles can be especially difficult to pinpoint at times. The only thing to do was jump in the vehicle in the evening, drive around the lake and determine exactly where they were. After checking out a few spots, I hit pay dirt.

Driving into one of our state parks, the big birds gave themselves away. Gobbles reverberated from the tree tops about 50 yards up a trail. Reveling in the "gold" just struck, my next morning's hunt was planned. Sleep was hard to come by later as adventure in a new spot awaited.

Arriving plenty early, quietly walking into the park, setting up and nestling in my chosen clump of trees, my shotgun was at the ready. My ears strained to hear the first soft yelp from the trees. The world stopped when the first gobble thundered from the treetops. From then on the air was full of exciting yelps and gobbles, reaching a crescendo which shattered my calm. Suddenly, the sound of huge wings beating hit my ears. A hen flew out of nowhere and landed 20 feet from me. Another and another joined her until I had 13 hens no more than 10 feet away, right in my lap. "Be still, my heart," I thought, swearing they could hear my heart beating. More hens were still flying down, giving me quite a show, while I wondered where the big boys were. Waiting was short-lived. I sensed different movement to the left. Thinking my eyeballs would make a noise if I even slightly moved them, I started shaking.

Here came my prize, not one, not two, but three nice gobblers, adding to the extravaganza. They had one thing on their minds which was to take out my Pretty Boy decoy and have all the hens to themselves. Their path never wavered and they never broke rank as they inched closer to Pretty Boy. There was time to size them up and choose the largest one, a tactic practiced by my Ol' Uncle Don.

The show was spectacular. I loved it. Never before had this wonderful amount of birds been in this close proximity to me. However, the time had come. The show needed a finale. The shot must have echoed up and down across the lake. I don't know because I didn't hear it. My chosen gobbler hit the ground. Mass confusion reigned as birds flew everywhere. My whoops and hollers never seemed to quit.

Never thinking a spectacle like this would be presented in my "own backyard," thanks was given for the game, the opportunity and nature. Lest I sound over dramatic, I must say it was such a textbook classic hunt with all those birds at my fingertips, it felt like a religious experience.

My prize was an Eastern/Merriam's hybrid and weighed 23 pounds. With a 10-inch beard and over inch-long spurs, he was a beauty to behold. That beauty now graces our living room and the hunt is relived, over and over. Every "trip" through the hunt brings a smile to my face.

The Pickerel Lake gobbler lives in the author's living room, providing reruns of the classic hunt.

CHAPTER THIRTY-THREE

OL' UNCLE DON
AND THE SLOUGH

It was a text book hunt with one exception. It was an "Ol' Uncle Don" hunt which means another weird adventure including a wet gobbler and soaked guide.

After putting birds to bed the night before, we were anxious to see how the morning hunt would pan out. The hunt was perfect, at least for awhile. Birds flew down and were behind trees about 70 yards from us. After softly calling, my box call was needed to get a tom's attention. It worked.

When the tom who answered me was finished with his harem, he decided to find the lone caller on the other side of the trees. Ol' Uncle Don's shot was true and the tom lay on the ground. We high-fived and thought "our team" was perfection. Suddenly, our eyes caught movement.

The gobbler had recovered and started to walk down the small tree line hiding a small slough. Uncle Don took another shot, missed, and took another. It connected. The impact lifted the gobbler up a couple feet and threw him backwards into the slough.

We rushed over to fish the dead bird out, but there was just enough of a breeze to float him away from the shore. Stepping in the water to reach out and grab him, a slippery moss-covered rock changed my procedure. Face first in the pond scum water was a very wet shock to my system, to say the least. When I finally hit solid ground, I looked up and Uncle Don was holding his sides and trying to keep a straight face. Meanwhile, the bird continued to float away to the opposite side of the slough.

Our only choice of retrieval was to walk around the tree line, up a path and finally reach the other side of the slough. The bird was indeed closer, but he was stuck in old cattails ten yards from shore and wouldn't move.

Our strategy was to find a very long branch that I could handle in the water and try to snag Uncle Don's prize. We found a good sized branch but it didn't work for us. It was too long and too heavy to hold up and over the water. It finally dropped into the slough. The only recourse was to walk in the water and get the bird—me, of course, not him. I was completely wet anyway, so in I ventured.

The slough bottom was again slippery. I sunk a couple inches in the mud and old cattail leaves tried to trip me when they wound around my ankles. It was very slow going, but I made headway. When the water was almost up to my shoulders, I finally made contact with the elusive floating branch and the bird. Turning the branch just right, the bird caught and I slowly dragged him back to me. I wouldn't look at Ol' Uncle Don's face when I handed him his wet trophy because I knew he'd be hiding a belly laugh and if I saw it, I'd probably smack him. All was quiet in the woods on the way back to the vehicle.

Giving thanks for living within a couple miles of the slough, the speed limit was ignored on the ride home. Sitting on a tarp to protect the car seats, the unpleasant pungent odor of pond scum and plant decay coming from me and the bird was overwhelming. Upon arrival at home, my boots were the only clothing item to come off before I ran into the shower--the first time shower water ever hit me while fully clothed.

Needless to say, both the bird and the guide looked like drowned rats. So ends the saga of Ol' Uncle Don and his bird in the slough. I think I still hear him laughing.

CHAPTER THIRTY-FOUR

AVOIDING THE CLANK

Even after turkey hunting and working in the industry for twenty years, one can still feel the pangs of intimidation. Hearing I was to hunt with celebrated turkey caller Ernie Calandrelli made me apprehensive about my capabilities.

AGLOW (Association of Great Lakes Outdoor Writers) held a turkey hunting event in western New York one spring and Calandrelli was to be my guide. He has been in the industry for over four decades and is Director of Public Relations and Advertising for Quaker Boy Game Calls in Orchard Park, New York. I needn't have worried about feelings of inferiority. Ernie is a great, down-to-earth, friendly and humorous guy. Although we ended up with an empty bag, it was one of the most memorable hunts of my turkey hunting trips. It was exciting even before the possibility of us landing in jail.

We met at a social hour the evening before the hunt and Ernie relayed all the hunting plans. After grabbing coffee at zero-dark-thirty the next morning, we were on our way to our lucky spot in New York's beautiful farm country.

After parking the vehicle on the side of a small gravel road, we trekked across a wheat field to the tree claim in which we'd set up. There was no action except some good stories and calling lessons from Ernie. After a time with no action, we walked again across another small field and settled in a spot among towering beech trees. I snuggled in between a couple trees as Ernie set up his decoys. Soon, his expert calling began in earnest, more aggressive this time.

Short sermons on patience were continually sprinkled between calling routines. I began to think "patience" was Ernie's middle name. Discussions on patience or lack thereof, was always a topic, illustrated by examples. I thought Ernie would be proud of me and the utmost patience I had always tried to practice while hunting. It was one of the first rules I learned and quickly saw how well it paid off.

Gobbles from our left stopped our conversation. Three jakes behind the trees were straining their throats to communicate with Ernie. The routine continued, Ernie using different calls to entice the birds around the "corner" from us. However, they never moved. They simply stood there repeating their throaty gobbles. Finally, all was quiet and we thought they were on the way in to us. Wrong. We practiced patience and not a feather or red head was to be seen. Finally, Ernie decided they had left and he suggested we call it a day. I agreed and he got up and walked over to pick up the decoys. We all know that is the time a lot of hunts go to heck and this was no different.

The jakes and Ernie simultaneously spotted and shocked each other. The birds were silently taking their own sweet time in coming to check us out by cautiously sneaking around trees bordering a small opening. I wasn't beside Ernie so I don't know if any blue words were uttered or not. He's probably too nice. You can't help but laugh in those situations and we did, especially when I asked him about his pontificating about "patience" for hours. We were time-strapped by then so had to leave.

The main adventure actually started on the way back to our vehicle. We rounded the first grouping of trees where we had first set up, walking back through the wheat field. It was a surprise to notice a pickup parked behind our vehicle and a gentleman standing on the edge of the field waiting for us. We became anxious as to what had happened. The closer we walked to the guy, the more pronounced his unhappy face appeared. We didn't understand the situation but we soon found out.

Questions were barked at us like "What do you think you are doing? Why are you here? Do you know this is private land? What gives you the right to be here?" Oh, oh. Then, a deputy sheriff drove up and asked why we were violating the law. Gulp. "Yes, I called the sheriff and the game warden," the irate landowner barked.

With shaking knees, I watched Ernie tactfully explain the situation. Ernie had been told he had the proper permission for where to hunt, where to park, what fields to cross and what trees in which to set up. There was a public trail for access on the far side of the trees, but we were told not to use it as it was too muddy. Obviously, we were misinformed. How embarrassing. The loud clank of jail cell doors echoed in Ernie's and my minds.

The irate gentleman told us he was surprised he found "people of your ages breaking the law." He obviously thought we were antiques. He had expected young people to be the culprits. The fact even made him angrier and he pontificated more. (Well, we weren't happy with our ages, either, but nothing we could do about it.) Telling him exactly who Ernie was, an elite representative for a host company for us outdoor writers at our event there in New York, and that I was a member of AGLOW didn't help much. We heard the "clank" again.

After a thorough verbal thrashing from the guy, we again explained what had transpired. After finally calming down, he listened. We did not knowingly trespass. We were told we had permission. Neither one of us would ever have walked across the farmer's field or hunted there had we not had permission. No way.

The conversation lightened up following the explanation of how careful Ernie was in seeking permission and the experiences I've had as a landowner myself and working with the South Dakota Game Fish and Parks Conservation Officers. He then mentioned the fact his daughters hunt—a perfect in for me to tell him about my first book, *Woman's Guide to Hunting.* I promised he'd receive a book from me and Ernie promised to send some turkey calls. We finally peacefully departed on a friendly, albeit shaky, basis. The trip back to town was rather quiet, both Ernie and I thanking our lucky stars we didn't hear the "clank."

However, we did have some giggles over being chewed out for our ages.

Although there were no birds in our bag, it was an unforgettable adventure. Ernie did a good job trying to deflect teasing away from us at the social hour that evening by deep frying walleye cheeks. Delicious!

Ernie is great. He kept me jail-free AND is a fantastic cook.

*Ernie Calandrelli is a celebrated turkey caller,
hunter and Director of Public Relations
and Advertising for Quaker Boy
Game Calls in New York.*

CHAPTER THIRTY-FIVE

MENTOR HUNT

Terry Helms lives down the beach from us at Pickerel Lake and we've known each other for decades. He looked apprehensive when he approached me and said he had to ask a favor. His grandson, Carson, had a burning desire to spring turkey hunt. Since Carson was only 10 years old at the time, he could qualify for the new mentor program South Dakota Game, Fish and Parks Department offered. He needed a mentor and grandpa Terry fit the bill. But, Terry knew nothing about turkey hunting.

Terry joked as he came into our house, but I knew he was on a mission. While gazing at a couple of mounted gobblers in our living room, he asked, "Could you guide Carson on a mentored turkey hunt? I'll be the mentor but you have to guide us."

I love taking new hunters out and introducing them to any kind of hunting and this was a very special invitation. He didn't have to twist my arm to receive an offer of introducing both grandfather and grandson to the wonders, and sometimes, the frustrations, of spring turkey hunting in northeast South Dakota. Of course, the answer was "yes."

The first step the elder Helms took was applying for a mentor license, and then a hunting clothing list ensued. Both hunters needed to be properly outfitted for our spring's unpredictable weather. "Turkey hunting class," the first required event on my teaching list, was the next step.

After an explanation of shotgun safety and with Grandpa looking on, Carson participated in simulated spring gobbler hunts in my living room. This "practice hunt" helps the new hunter learn what to usually (key word here is "usually") expect during the real hunt. All of my "students" must "graduate" from turkey hunting school before stepping foot in the turkey woods.

Carson Helms practicing aiming during pre-hunt turkey class in author's living room.

A late afternoon hunt on a warm sunny day started the adventure for Carson. A good friend of mine loves to have young first-time hunters hunt his land and welcomes them warmly.

We set up in a convenient spot turkeys frequent on their way to roost. Carson was ready. A small flock of the wily birds spotted us as we set up, and they took off in the opposite direction. We heard some yelping from behind us and to the left, then all was quiet for some time while Carson was learning to sit very still.

Carson soon turned to me. "There's one there," he whispered. As we slowly turned our heads to look, a big gobbler with a nice beard was standing 30 yards to our left, watching us. Instantly, the long-beard turned and ran.

As big gobblers usually are, this old bird was smart and was in a non-shooting zone for us. After the first day, the score was turkeys one, hunters zero. This meant the alarm would ring very early the next morning. Both grandpa and grandson were shocked when I announced a departure time of 4:00 a.m. for the next morning, but they were ready.

The morning hunt started with a muddy trek in the dark through a pasture, adjusting gates and try-ing not to trip on rocks on the way to a ground blind.

After setting my full strut Pretty Boy decoy up in front of the blind with a real hen decoy nearby, all we had to do was wait for the birds to wake up.

After a couple naps, Carson's eyes lighted up when he heard the first gobble. We watched the hormone-filled circus following the birds' fly down, hoping it wouldn't take too long for the toms to look elsewhere to find a hen. However, they were in no hurry and Carson learned patience is a big part of hunting. Meanwhile, Grandpa Terry was fretting over a lost hearing aid.

Before long, the flock started separating. Interestingly, two big toms were parading exactly where we had been set up the evening before. Turkeys also know how to exact revenge and laugh at hunters, which was another important lesson both rookie turkey hunters had to learn.

Soon, a huge hen showed up about 100 yards away. The hen answered my calls, spied the hen decoy and was on its way toward us. Between the hen's yelping and my yelping, we made enough racket to grab the attention of one of the strutting toms.

Carson's eyes grew large as he watched the ceremony unfold before him. Demanding he not move, I was ecstatic to have a live hen as a decoy to help us. Carson sat still as the big gobbler rambled toward us and it wasn't long before the big bird quickly challenged Pretty Boy.

Dancing, drumming, strutting and showing off, the gobbler was completely unaware of its future. After I made sure Carson was presented the show, I quietly whispered, "Shoot him where I told you."

The bird presented a perfect shot at about 12 yards. Carson pulled the trigger and the gobbler folded.

"Great shot, Carson," Grandpa Terry yelled and laughed. "I watched Carson make the shot. He pulled the trigger and the recoil threw him back a bit." Did Carson notice? Not at all.

Amid high-fives and congratulations, a happy crew blew out of the blind. The beautiful bird was a real trophy, especially for a young hunter's first bird. The mostly Merriam's bird (many in the area are Eastern-Merriam's hybrids) tipped the scale at 24 pounds. He had an 8.8-inch beard and over one-inch spurs.

Carson earned a gobbler feather for his cap and Grandpa was happy, too. He witnessed his grandson's first turkey hunt and was able to find his missing hearing aid. It was quite a successful morning.

Left, proud Grandfather Terry Helms.
Right, new turkey hunter Carson Helms.

CHAPTER THIRTY-SIX

THE TWO-MINUTE HUNT

My friend and hunting host, Truman Nelson, talks a lot about his "shooting house." Looking like a double-duty outhouse on wheels resting on the prairie, the shooting house is a perfect blind. Many deer have been shot from that wonderful vantage point in Truman's pasture. Now I'm having fun adding turkeys to the list.

Wildlife trails surround the shooting house and it's a wonderful place to simply observe wildlife. Best of all, action in the shooting house and its area is monitored through the big kitchen window on Truman's farm. More than once, I wished I had been in that big blind as we watched turkeys sauntering within shooting distance of it.

The morning I had my first chance to hunt in that glorious blind was almost a disaster. You know Murphy's Law and perfect planning. Two alarm clocks were set to assure me of a proper time to get up the next morning, get ready and drive to Truman's.

Unfortunately, at 6:00 a.m. while I'm still in bed, my husband yells into the bedroom, "Weren't you hunting this morning?" Yikes. Neither alarm went off.

I had promised Truman I'd be there at 6:00 a.m. for him to drive me and my gear out to the shooting house. How embarrassing. When I breathlessly stumbled into his kitchen at 6:45 or so, he and his son-in-law, Calvin Finnesand, laughed and thoroughly enjoyed my blunder.

The hunting plan was simple, but it had to follow the turkey's time table. Their routine included nesting in trees in a pasture to the east of the shooting house. When they were ready, they would take off and the entire flock would parade to the west, quite close to the shooting house on their way out to feed. My plan was to be set up in the "blind" to intercept a nice gobbler in the pack.

Because of my late start, we could see from the farm house the birds were already on their way. Disappointment sunk my shoulders. I had a perfect chance to bag a nice one and I blew it—or my alarms did. However, Truman said the birds were so intent on going to their regular feeding grounds they wouldn't be bothered by a vehicle coming out to the shooting house to unload decoys, etc. I took the chance and my luck changed.

We threw my gear in the shooting house and Truman even helped me by setting up Lena, my real stuffed hen decoy. I thought he had it in the wrong place, but I didn't have time, or the heart, to say anything. Turned out, it was a perfect setting. Truman raced back to the farm house and I quickly jumped into the shooting house while keeping an eye on the birds. They had simply stood and watched us and then continued on their way in my direction after Truman left.

As I injected the shells in my shotgun and looked up to see the birds, it was shocking to see three huge toms running, not walking, to my decoys. A window wasn't even open yet for shooting. Turning around, opening the window and getting the gun up was done in a flash. The three toms played ring-around-the-rosie beside Lena. Suddenly, one could not resist Lena's charms any longer and jumped on top of her. That would not do! Lena cost me $125 and she dare not get ruined. I clicked my tongue and the birds stopped for a split second. My shot echoed over the prairie and the dastardly bird was down.

Catching my breath and wondering how all that happened so fast, a dust cloud appeared in the pasture. Truman had watched it all from his kitchen table and his generous "chauffeur service" appeared at the shooting house.

Laughing, he took some photos and we celebrated back at the farm house with coffee. The fast and furious "two-minute" bird will always remain a fun hunting memory for both of us. Maybe it paid off to oversleep after all.

CHAPTER THIRTY-SEVEN

FUNKY CHICKEN HUNT

They were advertised in outdoor catalogs but looked so goofy I didn't want to spend money on one. However, after the spring 2016 hunt, I ran to the catalogs. The Funky Chicken is now part of my entourage with the rest of my turkey hunting gear.

My turkey hunting buddy, Robin Matushin, lives in Minnesota and had a rough time trying to find a weekend in 2016 to hunt tribal land in northeast South Dakota with me. After her son's wedding, a bout with strep throat and more, she made it here for the very last weekend of the season. Believing gobblers don't respond at season's end, we usually only hunt the first weeks of the season. We were explicitly proven wrong.

When Robin showed up on my doorstep, she had to show me the gift her kids gave her the previous Christmas. Laughing, she pulled the ugly weird decoy out of her vehicle. Being an extremely skinny-bodied jake with an oversized, tall and skinny neck and head, it was hilarious.

"It works," she exclaimed. "Two guys at work borrowed it, used it in Wisconsin, and each one brought home a gobbler." Well, willing to try anything new and having fun by simply being together in the turkey woods sounded good to me.

Our first setup the next morning was not fruitful. The great expectations we had for the new decoy did not pan out. We only set up the skinny bird, nothing else. We heard gobbling in the morning, but the toms followed their girlfriends in the opposite direction. Trying a few more good spots throughout the afternoon and evening, nothing worked. We did get our visiting done, though, and got caught up on each other's families. As Robin says, "I don't care if we don't see or get anything, it's just fun being here."

The next morning, we set up beside a fence adjacent to a small newly-sprouted corn field. Farm implements were lined up by the fence, making a natural hiding place for us, but yet with good visibility. The area we sat in was grass for 30 yards across before it steeply dropped down into a streambed. We joked and were having fun when a jake's gobble rattled nearby. We still laugh when recalling the poor confused jake who sauntered in to inspect the goofy decoy.

He slowly walked up to the weird bird, swinging his head to and fro, trying to figure out what he was looking at. He circled the decoy, stood and stared at it and walked around it some more. Many funny quotations floated in our heads as we watched the poor jake. Walking around to the backside of the decoy, the jake poked his head down underneath the decoy and tried to look up. He was trying to find the "bunghole." He just didn't know what this stupid bird was. We didn't want to move to record the session on our phones as we were rolling with laughter already, just watching. We whispered hilarious quotes to each other about what we thought the jake was thinking. We swear we could see the questionable look on his face. He just didn't know what the decoy really was.

After circling the decoy again a few times, he stopped dead on in front of it, beak to beak. And then he kissed the decoy. We just about lost it and gave ourselves away. Becoming bored with his newfound friend, the jake walked down the ridge and disappeared, leaving us with our sides hurting. We could not pull the trigger on him because he had presented us with such a good show.

We set up in the same place for the last hunt in the 2016 season that evening. Not knowing the whereabouts of our entertaining jake, we wondered if he'd come back. After a few lonesome hen calls from my slate, gobbles reverberated over the field to my left. Slowly moving my head, I saw him. He had a perfectly formed tail fanned out and connected to a huge black ball with a red head. The Merriam's/ Eastern cross stood and gobbled about 120 yards away. Walking slowly and rounding the fence corner on his way to us, I was shocked he was coming in to check out the dumb-looking decoy. His smaller buddy brought up the rear.

Communicating with only my eye movement, Robin got the message something was coming. However, she was seated partially behind an imple-ment tire and could not see the birds. It was so frus-trating to me she couldn't see them as they were definitely on a mission and were so beautiful in the setting sun. Robin knew she didn't dare move. She is a good hunter and I knew she'd connect when they came into her shooting alley.

Robin later said, "I was shaking while waiting for the gobbler to get close. I couldn't see him, but I knew he was close." Finally, she inched her head to the side just enough so she could spot him. She kept her eyes on the big guy as he delicately walked around the goofy decoy, inspecting this "mistake of nature." In a moment, Robin's trophy was on the ground. Another victory for Funky Chicken! Three in a row. He proved his worth yet again, and on the last day of the season. Holding my breath while I watched the pair approach the decoy, I still couldn't help laughing. Watching this big majestic bird com-ing in to the stupid-looking decoy was hilarious and unbelievable. And I thought my real mounted hen, Lena, was the best magnet, ever. What a shock this was.

Waiting until Robin took her shot, I fired at the second bird. Seeing his mentor on the ground, my smaller target rapidly scurried over the ridge, dodging my shot. I was excited as Robin connected, and was still laughing, ultimately not shooting straight. But no worries. We proved the strange new decoy really does work. And, we had a lot of fun doing it.

*Robin Matushin, Funky Chicken
and her trophy tom.*

CHAPTER THIRTY-EIGHT

ARNIE'S REQUEST

Arnie Goldade of Aberdeen, South Dakota, the first-time turkey hunter mentioned in Chapter 15, departed this world in November of 2016. He was a good friend of mine, friend of natural resources and a conservationist who put his money where his mouth was. He and his wife, Lori, worked tirelessly for every conservation organization in our area. The last request Arnie had of me was to take Lori spring wild turkey hunting the spring of 2017.

Mentoring Lori many years ago was a special experience and she had not hunted turkeys since our excursion to western South Dakota a few years later. Of course, I said, "yes," to Arnie's request. Application time approached and I reminded Lori to apply for a license. She was lucky and received a 2017 spring turkey tag for northeast South Dakota.

Plans were underway for the Arnie Goldade Memorial Turkey Hunt.

When time is limited for a hunt but yet a good experience is desired, I have the perfect hunting area. Birds come and go throughout the day from various directions and the success ratio is quite high, if hunting from the correct place. The turkey hunting gods were with Lori and I as we stepped into a permanently parked livestock trailer.

Our landowner host had generously placed chairs in the trailer for us, making a good resting place for my calls and gear. As we pulled the door closed behind us, excitement was reflected in Lori's eyes. When we were settled and agreed upon shooting alleys, it was time to call.

Livestock trailers make perfect blinds. There is a 350-degree visionary advantage, movement is not restricted, there are spaces to peek out from and "shotgun slots" to allow shooting from any direction.

Getting our bearings and surveying the situation and landscape led to reminiscing and fun conversation. After intermittent calling, gobblers and jakes appeared on the edge of the pasture, 250 yards away, up the ridge from a big gully with trees and a flowing stream. I continued calling aggressively. Sure enough, they behaved as we desired and starting walking toward us.

Lori had her pick of which slot in the trailer to shoot from, depending on which side of the trailer the birds chose to walk. Our eyes widened as the birds never wavered from their destination—us. They reached an intersection of fence lines and chose the correct fence line which would bring them right in front of Lori.

Although it was thin, the first bird sported a five-inch beard. Holding the bead of her shotgun on the turkey's head, she asked if it was OK with me if she shot a jake. "Of course," I told her, "they make the best meal." Boom! The shot echoed through the walls of the trailer and her bird was down. She is just as great a shot as ever.

As we walked over and picked up the bird, we were laughing, saying how much Arnie was probably looking down and laughing and shaking his head saying, "Gee whiz, they had to take a jake."

Lori was pleased with her prize as this was her first turkey in about 20 years. We know Arnie was really proud of her and glad we had honored him and his memory by hunting 2017 spring turkeys in his name, being successful and knowing Lori and I enjoyed the reunion of two hunting buddies.

*Lori Goldade and her prize
at the Arnie Goldade Memorial Turkey Hunt.*

CHAPTER THIRTY-NINE

A LUCKY DAY WITH TRIPLETS

Good Ol' Uncle Don had just celebrated his 86th birthday a week before the spring 2017 turkey season opened. We stayed in contact throughout the winter and I knew he was still in darn good shape. Consequently, another adventure of chasing gobblers together was on the calendar. His grandson, Jess Osborne, is a fan of the season and our hunt would again include him.

You have read about the goofy and funny experiences Ol' Uncle Don and I have under our belts and I looked forward to experiencing another one. After scouting my hunting area and feeling we'd have a good chance of finding birds, the weekend of the hunt arrived.

We started with an evening hunt near our home at Pickerel Lake. Although we neither saw nor heard any birds in the particular place I wanted to go, I figured we'd have a good chance if we stuck it out until sunset. Wrong.

There had been a terrible ice storm in December at the lake, downing many trees and electric poles. I hadn't known about all the brush and downed tree limbs and branches covering my proposed hunting site. Thinking it wouldn't be as bad to walk through as it looked, we still decided to make our way through to a good resting spot. We stumbled to a couple of trees and set up. (Jess was smarter and was perched up a hill.) Upon searching around us, I didn't think any self-respecting turkey would want to saunter through that little area when 20 yards away was a clear pasture. When contemplating moving, we were stopped short by hen clucks. Moving now was out of the question.

Mrs. Hen walked the periphery, peeking through the brush at the decoy, yelping and walking back and forth. She decided it wasn't worth fighting the deadfall to look at a decoy and she left. With ears straining to hear a gobble and rewarded only with silence, we were ready to call it quits. When gathering up my calls, we heard it—a faint gobble far away on top of the ridge above us. I revved up my loudest box call to get his attention but only hens appeared, walking left to right above us. But then, sneaking in like a ghost, the gobbler soon showed his colors as he pranced around with his girlfriends. Why would he answer me when he was having his pick of the harem beside him? At least we were treated to a nature show and it was quite a parade. I could feel the laughter in the gobbler's beady eyes as he looked down the ridge at us. Not wanting to chase the flock away from the area, we stayed put until the birds sashayed off to their roost. We left thinking, "wait until tomorrow, boy, you have it coming!"

Uncle Don knows the value of getting up at zero-dark-thirty to hunt turkeys, but it's getting harder for him to roll out of bed that early. Heck, it's getting harder for me, too. We ultimately planned an afternoon hunt for the next day. I know birds are always walking through trails near the beloved livestock trailer where Lori and I had hunted so I wanted to try hunting there again.

Uncle Don had a turkey tag for a different area so he was with us just for fun. Jess and I left him in a spot about 100 yards away from the livestock trailer. We told him to listen for our shots and we left to set up. I hadn't seen Jess for a year and we had fun discussing and cussing things while we waited for birds to show up. I knew there were big gobblers in the area so I used my Pretty Boy decoy. It didn't take long before we spotted big birds about 200 yards away. Again, the trusty box call got their attention.

A flock of seven, including gobblers, jakes and hens made their way to us via a fence line. Only calling sporadically to keep their attention, we waited with baited breath, shotguns at the ready. They came to a fence line intersection and paused to assess the situation. Five of the turkeys continued on walking to our left, but two birds decided to come our way and easily walked in front of us. Making sure Jess was ready to shoot, I told him, "on three, you take one on left and I'll get the one on the right." I whispered, "one..." and BOOM. Jess was a little too excited but he had a bird down. I took a shot at the one on the right, but I shot too late and he ran off.

Jess ran out and dragged a very large jake over to the trailer. "It's the best meat,

you know," he said. We decided to wait a while and see if more birds would show up so I could have a chance. It didn't take long. Jess told me to grab my binocular and check out "a black thing" way off in the woods on the opposite side of the livestock trailer.

Sure enough, it was a lone tom and he appeared to be huge. I got the box call fired up again and watched him walk toward us from about 200 yards. He wasn't in a hurry but he was steadily coming. The closer he became, the larger he appeared. He took his time so I tried to calm down, too.

The remaining group of five birds was hanging out about 80 yards from us and it looked like "my" gobbler would join up with them. Suddenly, we heard loud yelping from the vicinity where we left Uncle Don. Jess and I looked at each other with the same questioning expression, "is that Uncle Don?" As we listened some more, we were positive it was him. We had forgotten to tell him NOT to use his new yelper call! Well, he continued on, and sure enough, the birds wanted to investigate. "My" gobbler joined up with the group who had forgotten about Jess and me and proceeded to check out Uncle Don. Grrrrr.

That is when my box call received the workout of a lifetime—trying to draw those birds back to us. Lucky for us, Uncle Don must have moved his legs or something as the birds immediately stopped, turned around and started running to the livestock trailer. I quit calling, quickly grabbed my gun and placed it through a slot in the trailer. They were approaching fast and didn't stop when they heard my mouth call. "My" gobbler was leading the pack and I had to shoot in a hurry. There was no time to think. Boom! Now, the gobbler was officially mine.

Two birds taken by the livestock trailer in one afternoon—it was thrilling. We congratulated ourselves and relived both hunts when Uncle Don showed up. When asked about his yelping, Uncle Don first said he'd been sleeping and jumped awake when he heard our first two shots. Then he had decided to try out his new call, to our disdain.

After taking photos and retelling the stories, we made a plan for Uncle Don in his hunting unit for that evening. We set up in the same area as the evening before, only this time we were on top of the ridge. Cover was slight. The two of us sat by skinny twin trees, me behind Uncle Don with my legs hanging down over a cliff. Using Pretty Boy again, we gauged where we thought the birds would come from, based on the evening before. Because of no cover, Jess sat down below the ridge this time.

My trusty box call and two different glass and slate calls did the trick. Before long, a lusty gobble echoed through the woods. He sounded close already. I only gave a couple clucks on my mouth call and stopped calling. A gobble came from behind me, to Uncle Don's left. This is the time when all breathing stops. Uncle Don's elbow nudged my arm. A few seconds passed and then "boom." Our strategy worked! Uncle Don had his gobbler. A group hug and jumping up and down is normal for us crazy turkey hunters. What a day! Three birds taken in two different hunting units in one day. And, we didn't have to get up at 3:30 a.m. to do it.

More importantly, Uncle Don, cousin Jess and I had a wonderful family hunt together. Yes, 2017 spring turkey hunting was a rip-roaring success.

Ol' Uncle Don Schornack,
Jess Osborne and the author

Ol' Uncle Don and author check out
his gobbler's 9-inch-plus beard

CHAPTER FORTY

NO-SHOOT SUSIE

This chronicle of wild turkey hunting stories would not be complete without the story about a "student" of mine who was sweet and open to learning in the beginning but became maddening, frustrating and unforgivable. Anyone who has ever taught anyone anything has not had a perfect record. My efforts to develop this person into a turkey hunter was doomed. "No-Shoot-Susie" heads the list of failures.

Susie was excited about my adventures in the outdoors and wanted to join me by first of all, learning to shoot. We had several lessons first with a BB gun, then graduated to a .22-caliber rifle. She thought it was fun and after shooting several rifles, became fond of my bull-barrel target shooting .22, a prize won during the Custer State Park Once-in-a-Lifetime Elk Raffle. Susie was eager for more so the shotguns came out. Turkey hunting had piqued her interest and she began asking me all about it. As with every new hunter of mine, lessons began in the living room. All went well and we were both excited for her first hunt.

We set up at the edge of my favorite rancher's pasture for an afternoon hunt. Susie seemed comfortable with the gun and was remembering most everything she had been told. After sitting for awhile, I glanced at her. It was hilarious. She was sitting there with her full face mask on, but it was crooked. It only covered one eye. She wore glasses and the left lens reflected the sunlight. How could a person not tell something was wrong? Giggling, I told her to fix it and do it right this time. She minded me and we sat uneventfully until sunset.

We decided to hunt again a few days later. We'd received a foot of snow, but, heck, snow doesn't stop spring gobblers. Susie and I set up close to a fence where birds saunter back and forth. We had pads on which to sit so we wouldn't get wet and the snow didn't seem to bother Susie. She managed to stay quiet and have her mask on correctly. Soon, a gobble answered my box call.

Looking eloquent with lavish iridescent colors against the white snow, the gobbler walked straight to us. When he was in range for a perfect shot, I whispered, "Shoot." Nothing. "Shoot." Nothing. Finally saying it louder, I tried a third "Shoot." And, still nothing. She simply sat there. The tom stopped, looked around and searched for a waiting hen that never showed herself. He became bored and walked off with no shot echoing through the trees.

When asked why she didn't shoot, the answer was, "I just couldn't. I froze." Trying to contain my temper, I kept asking her what her problem was. Obviously, I had not prepared her correctly. She kept answered, "Nothing. I just couldn't shoot."

The next afternoon was spent shooting the shotgun again, and again. When asked if she were more confident, the answer was, "Oh yes. I'm ready now." Plans were then made for another hunt.

After waiting until the snow melted, we gave it another try. We hunted a beautiful forested area with a flowing stream which we had to cross. Finding a good place to set up, decoys were placed, and so was Susie. I gave her all the positive reinforcement I could muster, made sure she was comfortable, mask correctly on again and her gun placed correctly. There was a hill to our left so I explicitly explained the birds would probably come down the hill to us. Sitting behind her somewhat to her left was a good vantage point for me as I could see her. My shotgun was in my lap this time, "just in case."

After calling with my box call and giving some sweet soft yelps on the glass slate, a gobbler answered. Keeping up the conversation for a bit, anxiety reigned supreme. "She better do it this time," I thought.

It was classic. The gobbler came all the way down the hill, on our side of the stream. He strutted for an unseen hen, gobbled and danced—all within shotgun range, right in front of Susie. Waiting for a shot became unbearable. He wasn't going to stand there in front of her forever. Out loud, I told her to shoot. Three times. Nothing. She just sat there. Not again! I'd had enough. My shot rang through the trees and the tom was down even though the plan did not include me filling my tag that day. The question was, what excuse would she use this time?

I needn't have wondered about it as it was the same. A sheepish smile and "I just couldn't shoot." Twice now. And this after hours of pre-hunt preparation and calling in another gobbler for her. Sometimes, a person knows when to quit and this was it for me. The crowning touch was when we returned to the vehicle and she said, "Oh, I'm so glad this is over. Now I can wash all these clothes and put them away and they won't be laying around."

Her new name, No-Shoot-Susie, fit her well.

*How could anyone pass up
a gorgeous guy like this Merriam's?*

CHAPTER FORTY-ONE

A GRANDNEPHEW HUNT

"Turkeys don't like me," my 11-year-old grand-nephew lamented on the way home from a birdless hunt.

I had not seen Tanner Eisenbeisz since he was about five years old. His dad, my nephew Ryan, told me Tanner is well read, researches wildlife, watches outdoor videos and knows a lot about wildlife. However, that was a gross understatement. Tanner is a remarkable kid. He surprised me with his knowledge from the time they came in the front door the evening before our hunt until he left for home.

"Turkey class" was on the schedule, even before dinner, and we got right to it. Tanner was an eager-to-learn student, soaking in everything. When finished, I was walking into the kitchen to prepare dinner when I stopped in my tracks. I swore there was a turkey in the living room. Quickly turning around to see what was going on, Tanner stood there with a satisfied grin on his face. He had made those authentic turkey hen yelps. No call, no mouth diaphragm, no nothing. Tanner made the yelps with his throat. Unbelievable. I had him yelp over and over again and marveled at his talent. Having not ever been in the turkey woods, it was fantastic for this kid to have perfected a mature hen yelp.

"I do it with my throat," he said, demonstrating. "Do this and try it." He laughed at my feeble attempt to imitate him. During our set-ups the next two days, he was invaluable. I no longer needed to drag along ten turkeys calls while hunting; I'd simply use Tanner.

Spring of 2018 was cold, late and unusual. So was turkey behavior. The flock we hunted was inseparable. Using Tanner's yelps and my calls, we just could not get a gobbler to break away from the large family. They gobbled at our calls and looked us over from 100-200 yards away but wouldn't make the move we needed. After the evening set-up with no action, I was so disappointed for Tanner. I wanted him to connect with a bird even more than he did.

Tanner grabbed a fishing rod and ran to the lake shore when we arrived home. He proceeded to tell me about his angling prowess, impressing me, of course. When speaking of needed patience during turkey hunting, he announced, "I am very patient. I fished for 12 hours straight last weekend and didn't get tired." From there, he shared his young life's view of angling.

"You know, I like teaching people how to fish," he proudly said. "I even taught an old guy how to fish when I was just six years old." He was constantly entertaining, all centered upon wildlife.

The next morning's hunt was more of the same non-movement by big gobblers. We set up in a different spot, but it didn't matter. Watching 26 beautiful gobblers playing with many hens was spectacular, but just one coming into us would have been a more beautiful sight. At least Tanner had the opportunity to observe turkey behavior, be it good or bad, for the first time. We reluctantly had to call it a morning and left to have breakfast in a small nearby town. On the way back to the lake, Tanner again had the opportunity to exercise his special turkey yelp.

Taking back roads home afforded us the opportunity to observe ponds teeming with ducks and geese. Tanner gave a running commentary on duck identification. We then spied a small flock of turkeys by the side of the road. We stopped close by and directed Tanner to roll down his window and perform his yelp. It worked again. A couple toms were stumbling over themselves running and gobbling. Tanner laughed. The same scenario presented itself further on down the road. Again, Tanner yelped. Silence. He yelped again. Silence. Disappointed, he shouted, "Gobble!" The birds were silent and that's when we heard the announcement from Tanner, "Turkeys don't like me." Immediately, one tom excitedly exploded into gobbles. A super big grin broke over Tanner's face. One way or another, he did get the birds to obey him.

The weekend hunt was the only time Tanner could hunt so it was disappointing to me the birds did not cooperate. If anyone deserved a gobbler, he did. His dad and I talked about hunting ethics, values, etc. We told him he had to pay his dues and he would be better off by learning many things before it all fell in place in front of him so easily. Tanner did understand. And, he impressed me again.

Many people have been my hunting guests or partners, all with different attitudes. A couple people surprised me with their bad attitude and behavior after not shooting a bird. They were completely immature about the entire episode. However, not Tanner. That young man had the best attitude I've ever seen in a kid. He was disappointed, sure, but he did not pout, complain or become negative. He was excited and pleased to have been in the outdoors, learning, experiencing and having fun. Sure, he'd wanted a bird, but it wasn't to be, and he understood that, which shows more maturity than some adults I've seen. Tanner sent a nice thank you note to me and included at the end, beside the drawn picture of a gobbler, was the statement, "I have paid my dues."

When asked what he aspires to do in life, Tanner's quick answer was "to be a hunting and fishing guide." No surprise there.

With all the worries in today's world concerning the future of our hunting heritage, we can rest easy with kids like Tanner. We simply need a lot more of them.

I am so looking forward to hunting again with Tanner, hoping the next time he will have some feathers, spurs and a beard in his bag. He already has a great attitude.

Tanner Eisenbeisz paid his dues in the 2018 season and is ready for 2019.

This Angus cow entertained Tanner when she fell in love with the Ugly Jake and wouldn't leave it alone.

*Tanner still has fun in the outdoors,
even when the turkeys do not cooperate.*

ADDENDUM I

WILD TURKEY BIOLOGY

Known as a big bird with a little brain, wild turkeys have a terrible reputation for being a dumb animal. However, if you've ever tried to hunt them, you probably know turkeys are anything but dumb.

One of the best ways to defend their smarts is to look at a turkey's vocabulary, which is comprised of 11 unique vocalizations, according to the Cornell University's Lab of Ornithology. Most animals make sounds, but a truly dumb animal wouldn't have the need or ability to produce such a complex range of sounds.

Their conservation success story also gains them intelligence points. In the early 20th century there were only about 30,000 wild turkeys left on the continent. Today, however, more than 7 million wild turkeys inhabit North America, according to population estimates from the National Wild Turkey Federation.

Much of this triumph is thanks to the turkey's smarts and ability to adapt, but it's also due to the advanced biological characteristics that help them survive on a daily basis, especially during hunting season.

Turkeys have some of the finest eyesight in the animal kingdom, which is a reputation they've had for a long time. With eyes on the side of their head, turkeys can see 270 degrees at any given time. When you consider how a turkey nervously bobs its head and rotates its neck, it's almost constantly taking in observing a full 360 degrees around it.

Most birds see in color, and turkeys are no exception, relying heavily on color vision to find mates and detect predators. Their eyes are composed of seven different types of photoreceptors and six different types of cones. For comparison, humans only have four different types of photoreceptors and three single cones.

One of the cones turkeys possess has spectral sensitivity to wavelengths near 400 nanometers, which falls in the UV-light range. This extended view of the color spectrum allows them to pick up things that human eyes can't, such as the phosphates in laundry detergent that create a bright, blue glow around otherwise camouflaged hunters who aren't mindful of their laundry habits.

What turkeys lack, though, is the ability to see well at night. The abundance of cones that allows them to see such detailed colors means their eyes lack rods, the visual cells associated with night vision. This is why turkeys are often overcautious with their roosting habits, flying to the treetops before the sun sets and then not flying down in the mornings until after first light.

The lack of low-light sight is why it's common for turkey hunters to set up really early in the morning, sometimes an hour or more before dawn. But this doesn't mean hunters can wander too close to the roost in the dark, because turkeys still have a great sense of hearing.

A wild turkey's ear biology is fairly similar to a human's, as it has an outer ear, middle ear and inner ear. A turkey's outer ear is the small hole in the side of its head, which is less efficient than a human ear at gathering sound due to the lack of pinna, which is the external part of the ear often associated with mammals—think of ear lobes. The purpose of pinna is to funnel and concentrate sound waves, something that turkeys struggle to do.

However, bird species also have a single structure of bone and cartilage called columella in their ears that dramatically speeds up how quickly they process sound. While humans hear sounds in bytes about 1/20 of a second long, columella helps birds process sound at up to 1/200 of a second. That gives turkeys the ability to hear much shorter notes, where one note to us equals 10 notes to them.

All that points to why hunters often fawn at great turkey calls and callers. The yelps and cuts you make on your turkey calls might sound spot on to you, but the masterful ears of a tom tell him otherwise.

If a turkey learns through visual or audible cues that something isn't right, it's likely they'll leap into flight. While flying may look like a real chore for turkeys, they're actually quite good at it. They're capable of going over a mile at a time by alternating wing beats and gliding.

They still have their limitations, though, and can only carry on with continuous wing beats for a couple hundred yards. Once they gain flight, they're capable of reaching speeds up to 50 mph.

As with pheasants, however, wild turkeys have a run-first, fly-second mentality and they've been documented running up to 25 mph.

There are a couple factors which help make turkeys ideal track stars. One of them is how their tendons are structured, and to better understand how turkeys cover so much ground, a study was done to observe the impact their leg tendons take when compressed. To do this, researchers dropped turkeys from 5 feet in the air and observed the landings with foil-strain gauges glued to the turkeys' legs.

Observers noted a turkey's tendons protect surrounding muscle fibers by absorbing energy from a hard landing before releasing it back to surrounding muscles more slowly. This process is perfect for a specimen that needs to make quick escapes or catapult itself into flight.

By Spencer Neuharth,
South Dakota Freelance Outdoor Writer

NATIONAL WILD TURKEY FEDERATION

Anyone interested in wild turkeys, for many reasons, should join the National Wild Turkey Federation. It is the only conservation organization in the country explicitly founded for the betterment of wild turkeys. The NWTF is dedicated to conserving the American wild turkey and preserving our hunting heritage. Through dynamic partnerships with state and federal wildlife agencies, NWTF and its members have helped restore wild turkey populations across the country.

With turkey populations established in 49 states (all except Alaska), NWTF is determined to Save the Habitat. Save the Hunt. It is an initiative that mobilizes science, fundraising and devoted volunteers to give NWTF more energy and purpose than ever.

Through the initiative, NWTF is committed to raising $1.2 billion to conserve or enhance more than four million acres of essential upland wildlife habitat, recruit 1.5 million hunters and open access to 500,000 acres for hunting, shooting and outdoor enjoyment.

When founded in 1973, there were about 1.5 million wild turkeys in North America. After decades of dedicated work, that number hit a historic high of almost 7 million turkeys thanks to tremendous efforts of dedicated volunteers, professional staff and committed partners.

The mission of NWTF is no less urgent today than when founded. What we do in coming decades will be instrumental in not only enhancing wild turkey populations, but also the continuation of hunting and improving habitat for countless other wildlife species.

If you hunt turkeys, love to watch them, are concerned about them and their habitat and want to know more, join a local chapter of the National Wild Turkey Federation. There are many chapters across South Dakota and the nation. See www.nwtf.org for wild turkey information and to find a chapter nearest you.

ADDENDUM II

Turkey hunting stories would not be complete in the absence of a couple delicious recipes. My family enjoys fettuccine so after some experimentation in the kitchen, the following recipe pleases their palates.

We also enjoy lean protein for snacks in this health-conscious world and wild turkey jerky fits the bill.

There are many ways to prepare and enjoy the fruits of a wild turkey hunt. These are simply my two favorites.

WILD TURKEY FETTUCCINI ALFREDO

Wild turkey breast:

Cook in crock pot on LOW with 2 cans of Chicken Broth soup for 7-8 hours for young bird, 10-15 hours on for older bird. Add favorite seasonings. Cool. Shred. Set aside.

Alfredo Sauce:

Sliced fresh mushrooms

1 small onion, chopped fine

3 cloves garlic, minced or pressed, or canned

3 ½ cups of Half & Half, or use ½ milk and ½ heavy cream.

1/4 cup finely chopped parsley

Salt and pepper

5 Tbsp olive oil, divided

1 Tbsp butter

1 tsp Italian seasoning

1 cup grated Parmesan cheese

1 jar Alfredo w/Parmesan cheese (Classico, etc.)

Angel Hair or fettuccini pasta

When meat is fully cooked, start sauce. In large skillet, (this is optional—if meat is done well, there is no need to sauté) heat 2 Tbsp olive oil over medium/high heat and sauté meat until light golden and cooked through (5 min.). Remove meat.

In same pan, same heat, heat 3 Tbsp olive oil and butter. Add onion and sauté 3 minutes, or until soft. Add sliced mushrooms, cover and sauté until soft (5-7 min), stirring frequently. Add garlic and sauté another 30 seconds, stirring constantly.

Add Half & Half or milk mixture and simmer over medium/high heat 5-7 minutes, or until just barely beginning to thicken. Add turkey meat back to the pan, with parsley, Parmesan cheese, jar of Alfredo sauce and season with salt and pepper, Italian seasoning. Simmer 15 minutes. Add milk if too thick.

Cook pasta, pour sauce over, serve. Enjoy!

HI MOUNTAIN
TURKEY JERKY

As is says on the box, making your own jerky at home is easy with Hi Mountain's Jerky Cure and Seasoning Kits. Wild game jerky is delicious and wild turkey jerky is a special treat.

Hi Mountain Jerky Kits are readily available in grocery stores, outdoor stores and online at www.himtnjerky.com. The kits contain everything you need to make this scrumptious snack, including explicit and easy directions. There is a myriad of flavors from which to choose. Our favorites are Mesquite and Pepper & Garlic. The best part is this jerky can be made in your kitchen oven.

Using a Food Saver to preserve the jerky in sealed plastic bags and then freezing them insures your turkey snacks will be fresh to enjoy for a long time—if they are not devoured in a few days.